GROWING UP ON CHRISTIAN 40

*To Dan
a Best Friend
& one of the presents
Love Eme*

EVELYN BURTCHEARD

outskirtspress

DENVER, COLORADO

Growing Up On Christian 40
All Rights Reserved.
Copyright © 2016 Evelyn Burtcheard
v1.0

Outskirts Press, Inc.
http://www.outskirtspress.com

ISBN: 978-1-4787-7369-6

Outskirts Press and the "OP" logo are trademarks belonging to Outskirts Press, Inc.

PRINTED IN THE UNITED STATES OF AMERICA

This book is written in memory of my parents Oscar and Lottie Pugh who through their Irish/Native American and Scottish ancestry taught me the values of family and that a person was only as good as their word. They taught me to value time and to always attempt to make the most of it; to love horses and nature that has been a life-long enjoyment.

I give enormous credit to Kim Drury and Dianne Cherry for their technical knowledge and support when my computer did its funky thing and I could not correct it. They saved this book. I am forever in your gratitude. Without your assistance and perseverance I would have had to retype the book again.

Table of Contents

Part I

1

Before Christian Forty

It seemed to me as I grew up in central Illinois most families had at least one kid that was naturally a one person demolition crew who all by themselves and all alone could do a fair amount of destruction. This kid (in my opinion) is one that strange, weird and funny things seem to happen to. In our family this person was my brother Donny. He caused all sorts of havoc by just being in the wrong place at the right time and made it appear reasonable. One may have difficulty seeing the reasoning at the time the incident is happening, especially if you are part of the big plan; and Donny always had a plan. At any time one could always find one's self walking in the company of disaster. Donny did not have to look for trouble it was always just one step away, no matter which way he turned. That is not to say Donny looked for trouble, just that it was always so, oh, so available.

An uncle gave Donny a Billy goat. If Mom and Dad had been asked about this gift I am pretty certain they would not have agreed. As it was, Uncle Frank arrived with the goat in the back of his truck and Donny fell in love with it. This goat was supposed to have been trained to drive and somewhere Donny got the idea it could be ridden. Don't all cowboys ride their trusty steeds? Donny was always in cowboy mode. His goat was the next best thing to a horse or a pony. For a time the goat pulled the wagon and Donny was never happier. However each time I tried to drive the critter he ran off with me or turned and shook his horns at me. As soon as I jumped out of the wagon he would return to eating grass. I never argued with him and he was not my favorite animal. I guess I just did not have Donny's voice of authority.

Donny was never one to leave well enough alone. He decided that if the goat could go fast alone, just think of how fast he could go if he had help from the dog. He hitched the goat to the wagon and proceeded to tie the dog alongside. Donny got into the wagon. The dog started barking. The goat started running. The goat ran up the steps of the front porch, across the porch and instead of going back down the steps, he decided to jump off. This might have worked EXCEPT the goat went one way around the porch post and the dog went the other. The wagon turned over spilling Donny out on the ground below. The dog and the goat were not happy to be tied together hanging from the porch post. Mom was most unhappy but somehow she got the pair untied and sent them on their way. I managed to find something else to occupy my time as the three wandered off on their own adventure, usually at someone else's expense.

～⌒⌒～

During this time Mom took Donny and me to Dads parents. My Grandmother had what is now called Alzheimer's disease; an illness that caused her to not recognize her family. She had daughters but she wanted Mom and Aunt Victoria, Tory Bell. So Mom and Aunt Tory moved to Granddad and Granny's home for the time before her death. Mom and Aunt Tory were both expecting babies, but of course I did not know that. Mom had to take Donny and me with her and we slept on pallets while we were there. Aunt Tory had sisters to help her but Mom did not. Mom and Aunt Tory hardly left the room. Donny and I were not allowed to leave the house because Granddad had a big yellow dog that had bitten some of the kids. He bit Donny in the face when Donny was two years old and left a terrible scar on his forehead. Granddad refused to pen the dog up. I do not know how long we were there but we came home after Granny died. Years later I wondered why her daughters did not help with her care, but Granny only wanted Mom or Aunt Tory.

In August of that year I turned six, Mom and Dad told me I was getting a special surprise. My birthday was the 4th of September and by all of the excitement I just knew the surprise would be a pony. I could hardly contain myself dreaming of my own horse. It didn't even have to be beautiful, just head, tail and four legs and I would be so happy.

The big day arrived but it was August 28th, well almost the 4th of September and I didn't really mind getting my pony early. Donny and I were told to stay seated on the front porch. This was strange shouldn't we be at the barn? By now Donny was excited also (I had to let him in on my secret) as we watched for a truck to come down the long drive to the house. As time passed I was certain my parents had forgotten my pony. There was a neighbor lady visiting and I thought Dad at least should be outside waiting with us ready to saddle my horse. We waited and waited and finally the neighbor lady brought me a small bundle, saying "here is your surprise, a baby brother!" A baby brother! I already had a brother and didn't think he was such a prize. Where was my horse or my pony? Of course I cried here was a baby not my horse!

Later Mom promised me that when I was big enough I would have a horse of my own. In the meantime I was expected to rock my surprise baby brother and dream of my own horse. The baby became a wonderful person for me to talk to and I told him of the great horses I would have someday. Daniel Leroy – Danny was the sweetest, happiest baby one could ever hope to care for. I almost forgot the horse, but not quite.

Donny, the goat and the dog and the wagon were always looking for something to do so they headed for the back yard of the house. (I don't think the goat even had a name. The name Dad called it would get your mouth washed with soap. I think perhaps my parents believed if it had no name it would just disappear.) I had been told to stay close by so that when the baby woke up I could tend to him. Mom couldn't stop with her canning just anytime, so my job was to play with Danny when he was awake. In the mean time I had a picture book to read. I was curled up in the rocker on the porch when the goat and dog came around the house again. Up the steps and onto the porch, with all the noise of a tornado, and Donny was right behind them yelling. The harness was a tangled mess and I tried to hush the three stooges but to no avail. Again I heard the baby start to cry.

Before we could get the animals apart Mom arrived very upset because the noise had awakened the baby. I was sent to rock him back to sleep while Mom got the dog and goat untangled again. As I sat rocking Danny I watched Donny leading his goat, the dog following alongside. Down the yard they went on their merry way, looking for another dumb idea to try. The goat swinging his head at the dog, the dog barking and Donny was marching along as if he had them both under control.

A few days later Donny and I went to feed the chickens and gather the eggs. He tied the goat, again hitched to the wagon, to the gate post. While we were occupied with the chickens the goat managed to set himself free. He chewed on everything. When the goat got loose the gate came open and the goat walked into the chicken yard pulling the wagon behind him. The goat alone was enough to scare the chickens however the rattle and banging of the wagon put the finishing touches to the scenario. Old hens that seldom made a peep squawked at the top of their lungs. The dog started to bark; the goat got excited and started to run only to get the wagon caught on a feeder. Chicken feathers were flying everywhere. Donny was laughing so hard he was useless and I was afraid of the goat. Mom must have thought she had been blessed with a couple of fools when she saw the mess we made in the chicken yard. At the time she muttered something about wishing she had never set eyes on that goat!

Not long after the chicken yard episode the goat realized that if he stood up on an old tree stump in the yard and kept turning to face

Donny, shaking his horns Donny could not slip the lead rope on him. After a while the goat would jump down and start to eat, and finally let Donny catch him, only to start their dumb routine over again. Donny declared this was fun until he tired of the sport and turned the goat free or got a hand full of chicken feed to distract the goat so he could put the harness on him.

Dad was hired to break horses that were rounded up and shipped to Illinois from Oklahoma. They were held in a solid high pole corral that they could not see over. When he was breaking horses it was THE LAW that we were never to go into the barn alone, only if mom or dad was with us. The horses spooked very badly and for some reason they did not understand little kids, having seen very few if any in their lifetime. I was at the back of the corral watching what I could see through the cracks between two poles as Dad had one of the horses out working with it.

Suddenly it sounded as if the whole barn exploded. The goat had gotten away from Donny and jumped over the lower half of the Dutch door into the hallway of the barn. From where the horses were, all they could see was the top half of the goat as he walked in front of the manger. The high manger kept the goat from just walking into where they were and getting to them. But no matter they wanted no part of him. All the excitement inside caused the horse outside to go crazy, (it does not take much to upset a range horse!) The next thing I saw was my Dad climbing over the top of the corral. The goat finally had all the fun he could stand and jumped back out the way he jumped in.

The next day Uncle Frank came and got the goat. I was really surprised that Donny was not upset to see the goat leave. It was later that I learned Donny had discovered that if he could catch a baby calf in the pen it would drag him for a short distance before he lost hold. He tried to convince me that it was really fun to be dragged and stepped on by these baby calves. For once I was smart enough not to be taken in by one of his schemes. I knew that when Dad and Mom found out about his riding the baby calves the joy would end right then and there. Dad walked into the barn lot one day while Donny was calf riding. And I was right it stopped but he went on to other exciting things.

When I started school we lived quite a distance from the school house. To get to the road we had to go down a long lane through two gates, past grazing cattle and sheep. The man Dad worked for had a big white faced red bull, Dad said he wasn't mean but Donny and I were not allowed to go through the gate into their pasture when they were in the front pasture.

Dad took me to the main road where I met four neighbor girls by the name of Moomey, Mary Lou, Carolyn Sue, Doris Elaine and Martha Jane. The girls were very good to me and brought me treats and walked me to and from school each day. I didn't finish the school year with them as we moved to Springfield.

After the bombing of Pearl Harbor by the Japanese on December 7, 1941 the factories were begging for workers. Dad could make so much more money in the factory than working for a farmer and break-ing horses, although there was still a demand for good broke horses. Dad got a job working at Allis-Chalmers in Springfield. I think Dad had all the breaking of wild horses he wanted, since he had done that type of work for several years. My parents sold our livestock and we moved to town, I started going to Matheny School on the south east side of Springfield.

I was lost in such a large school but I could see my home when I was outside at recess. I hated it when we had fire drills, I was afraid of heights and the big cylindrical slide was fearsome. However after I had gone down the big terrifying tube I could see my home across the cow pasture between the school and our home. Some of the kids thought it was fun and looked forward to the day set aside for the drill. But I certainly did not.

Dad had begun to work at Allis Chalmers of Springfield with Mom's brother Charlie. Uncle Charlie and his family lived a few blocks from us. My parents realized their mistake to move to town very soon after arriving. They had never lived in a big town before. They sat on the side porch of our home which faced the cow pasture and the school and enjoyed watching the cattle. Both my parents were country born and bred and they were very unhappy and homesick in the city. Mom's sister Vesta, her husband Floyd and son Ronald lived several blocks south of us and Mom took care of Ronny, even though Vesta didn't work. Floyd enlisted in the Navy and Aunt Vesta moved back to our grandparent's home west of Edinburg.

⁊⁊∾

One of the things school age kids are prone to do is bring home children's diseases. In my case it was chicken pox and Donny had them worse than I. I had a few on my chest while Donny had them so badly he could not walk. Danny was just a few months old and had spots on his beautiful baby face.

One day after school I started home but a group of older boys had piled bricks on each side of our street where a building had been torn down. I had to go down that street as it was the only safe way I could get home. Bricks were flying back and forth with much swearing and Mom was yelling for me to stay where I was. From behind me a young Negro woman took my hand and began yelling at the boys. They finally stopped fighting and she walked me home to a frantic thankful mother.

⁊⁊∾

Mom and Dad took the three of us children to Uncle Bucks home to help them do repairs on their house. Dad and Uncle Buck replaced the tar paper on the roof of the house and Mom cooked and cleaned. Mom and Aunt Clara were both expecting a baby but Aunt Clara spent most of her time in bed both the babies were almost due. Uncle Buck and Aunt Clara had five other children and their youngest child was about the same age as Danny. Florence, Delores and I were on a blanket in the front yard taking care of the babies Rita and Danny. Eddy Gene and Donny were off with the freedom that boys seemed to inherit.

Uncle Buck and Aunt Clara lived south of the Star School on a dead end road. There was nothing special I remember about their home but what would a six going on seven year old observe except I liked the country and the timber. Two accidents happened that I do very well remember. Everyone was busy, Dad and Uncle Buck were on the roof working, Eddy Gene and Donny were in the yard throwing a round metal disk from the end of the roll of tar paper. The disk would sail through the air, land, and the boys would race to where it landed and throw it again. Finally they both had disks throwing and running. They were supposed to be playing in the back yard however their disks took them everywhere. Visiting in the country it was great to have room to run and play and Donny was enjoying every minute of freedom.

Mom came out on the porch just as a disk sailed through the air. She later said she watched helplessly as the black round disk sailed from the sky straight towards those of us on the blanket with the babies. The disk made a swoop and struck me in the right side of my face on the cheek bone. I don't remember much after that except the pain and awful blood. The disk had just missed my right eye and cut a two inch long furrow into my cheek. The adults came running when I screamed and of course Danny and Rita cried and finally all of us girls were crying. Mom was trying to stop the bleeding while Dad and Uncle Buck wanted to know what happened. I was patched up and my eye swelled shut for a few days, but I did not have any further complications. There was no way of knowing which of the boys threw the disk so their "toys" were confiscated and they were sent to the back yard. It was an accident that I am certain the boys did not intend to hurt anyone. They were not vicious just very busy. The disk when thrown sort of had a mind of its own, going with the wind. In later years I never thought about the scar as I wasn't much for mirrors and the scar was something that was just there.

A day or two later, Dad and Uncle Buck were back on the roof of their house and Eddy Gene and Donny were off in the back yard which sloped down to a small creek. Suddenly a scream split the air and all the adults ran to the back yard. Again we girls were in the front yard with the babies, so we had to wait until someone told us what happened. As Eddy Gene and Donny went on their adventurous way Eddy Gene stepped into a broken canning jar and cut his foot badly. Now the families had two bandaged kids.

Little did my family know we were only a stone's throw from the property that would someday be known to us as our Christian Forty?

My parents were so unhappy living in town that we moved from Springfield very soon. Dad found a house several miles south east of Rochester in the country and we moved. There was a house and barn and some out buildings but we had no livestock. Donny and I dreamed of filling the barn with horses and cows even though there were no fences around the place. We liked our school and there were some neighbor kids to play with. For a time things were fine, But I think we all missed the livestock. Donny even talked about getting another goat which Mom and Dad certainly did not encourage.

～♪⟳～

The lady that lived at the end of our lane, and across the road became a very good friend to Mom and later was also my mother's midwife. Aunt Dora, as all the neighboring folks around called her was one of the sweetest ladies one could ever meet. She lived with her mother and brother and they all were very nice. However she and Donny did not hit it off. Aunt Dora raised geese and although they were inside a fenced pasture, the geese and Donny had a real love-hate relationship. Donny loved to tease them and they hated it! Aunt Dora had warned Donny about teasing the ganders, but of course that fell on deaf ears.

One morning as we were going to school Mom gave me a note to take to Aunt Dora. (We had no telephone) Since I would have to go a little out of my way I left before Donny did. Returning I passed our lane and I looked to see where Donny had taken himself off to. He was nowhere in sight. Thinking he had gone on to school I started to run to catch up with him. From behind me I heard a Banshee screech and squall! Turning around I saw Donny coming along the fence where Aunt Dora had the geese penned. One of the ganders had gotten out of the pen and while Donny was intent on teasing the geese in the pen the gander outside caught up with him!

I stood dumb-founded as Donny and goose raced past me as if I were invisible. When I caught up with Donny he was inspecting his legs that were covered with purple welts. The gander had gotten the best of him. For the rest of the time we lived there, Donny pretended to ignore the geese when they were in that particular pasture, and would march past with his head held high but I caught him looking at them out of the corner of his eye. This did not last very long since Donny had a short memory when it came to those geese.

∾୨ତ∾

Valentine's Day was a special day at our country school. Mom had helped us make Valentines for everyone in the school and the teacher. She kept colored paper (that was put away to be used only when she got it down) and we had our crayons and paints and it was a three or four day event to get our valentines made. Mom made cookies for the whole class. She packed our lunches, valentines and cookies in covered pails and as it became time for Dad to get home from work, he worked the third shift at Allis Chalmers in Springfield, we waited.

When the time came that we had to leave and Dad still wasn't home Mom sent us over to Aunt Dora's for her brother to take us to school. Off we went down the long lane with our goodies. Aunt Dora and her brother had a car and when Dad worked overtime and the weather was bad one of them would take us the mile or more to school. In turn Mom took Aunt Dora and her mother grocery shopping or their Doctors visits. The war had caused gasoline to be rationed and the neighbors would join together to save gasoline by taking as few trips to town as possible and going with one another. Each family had gas stamps and when they were gone the family had to wait until the next month or when they were issued again. Aunt Dora could drive but she said she liked to go with Mom. Aunt Dora said her brother and the car wasn't home and we should go back home and wait for him or Dad to get home.

When we got out in the road we decided it wasn't too cold to walk to school. It was cold and snowing off and on but the sun shined in between snow squalls and we were bundled up good. Donny didn't even bother to tease Aunt Dora's geese since we had a mission this day.

Off we went the mile or so to school. There were five or six kids already at school when we arrived, but the door was locked and we couldn't get in. The teacher's car wasn't there and no one knew where she was. We all stood around discussing the problem. Since Donny and I were among the younger kids we were impressed with the reason the older kids told us as to why we had no teacher. Finally a lady that lived across the drive from the school came over and told us the teacher was sick and there would be no school. We were told to go home. The big kids that lived east took off running for home.

Back up the road we trudged, happy for a day off from school but sad that we would have to wait for our Valentine party. We had gone about a half a mile when we both got tired and we were cold so we decided to sit down in the ditch for a while to rest. The next thing we knew someone was calling our names. A neighbor Mr. Truax was going by and saw us sitting in the ditch, asleep! He bundled us into his truck and took us home. Dad was home, he thought the neighbor Mr. Smith had taken us to school. Aunt Dora thought we had gone home like she told us to.

Mom was frantic when she realized what had happened. Donny and I both came down with colds. Mom mixed goose fat and mustard into a plaster that was tied to our chest and we were given hot honey cinnamon milk and put to bed. We were no worse for wear but we sure got a good talking to when Mom knew we were alright. I remember when Mom started using Vicks Vapor Rub, it was a great improvement over goose grease but I still didn't like it.

The next spring our family expected a new baby and there was much excitement. Danny was two years old and no longer a baby. The doctor arrived and we were surprised to see a woman doctor. "She ain't no doctor she's a woman!" Donny announced. Dad sat Donny, Danny and myself on the sofa and told us to stay out of the way. Aunt Dora arrived well before the doctor and she was busy in the room with Mom. We sat, slept and then after what seemed like hours later we finally heard a baby cry.

Donny jumped up with a shout that woke Danny, as Aunt Dora and Dad came into the living room. Dad moved a large overstuffed chair lined with pillows closer to the heating stove, and Aunt Dora placed the tiny bundle on the pillows in the chair. All three of us kids were staring wide eyed at the tiny red faced baby, when Aunt Dora brought in another baby. This one was crying at the top of his lungs, as she placed him in the chair and returned to the bed room.

Finally Aunt Dora returned to her charges in the chair in the living room. Donny with hands on hips and his chin jutted out, demanded, "Well where is the rest of them?" The kid was never satisfied. The babies were named Jarold Ray and Carold Jay.

They were really good babies but our parents were told very early that Carold was ill. He preferred to be left on the bed and watch the activity rather than be a part of it. Jarold or Jerry as we nicknamed him wanted to be in the midst of everything and Donny had fun pushing Jerry in his stroller. I am surprised the child did not become a race car driver, he learned very early what speed was, at least when Mom was out of the room.

There weren't any girls my age living close to us, but a family that lived north of us had a boy that was about Donny's age. He often came to our house to play.

On one occasion Mom sent me to the barn to tell the neighbor kid it was time for him to go home. The kid had arrived with a note in hand from his mother. He was known to "forget" the time he was supposed to go home. But on this day Mom made certain that the plan was clear.

The boys hid in the hay loft when they saw me coming from the house. Donny had the theory that if he didn't see you when he was told something, "then he didn't know about it, so it didn't count," but this only applied to me. He was smart enough not to try to use this dumb strategy on Mom or Dad.

I climbed up the ladder and as my head cleared the loft floor Donny shot at me with the neighbor kid's air rifle or more fondly called a b-b gun. They were not supposed to have the gun but the kid brought it along and hidden it in the ditch, until such a time as it was "needed". To use on Donny's sister I can only presume. Mom had washed my hair and made large rolled curls. The b-b lodged in a curl on the top of my head. Donny was in a lot of trouble when Mom combed my hair and the b-b fell to the floor. The neighbor kid was not allowed to play at our house for a long time which was fine with me.

∽◦◦

Autumn and spring was my most favorite time of year. We would play outside until the weather got so cold we quit playing outside bare-footed and neither one of us like shoes. I loved to play outside until it got dark, Mom put lights on in the house and the train that ran paral-lel to Route 29 and was a couple of miles north of our house blew the long sorrowful melancholy whistle as if to say playtime was over. It was almost the signal for us to go in for supper. Strange how such mundane happenings can bring back memories. I think about but do not dwell on the train whistle each time I hear it today.

Part II

2

The Move to Christian Forty

One year and one week after the twins were born, the smaller of the two babies passed away in his sleep. The doctors told Mom and Dad when the babies were born that Carold Jay had a heart problem they could not repair. They called his condition a "blue baby" and he was not as active as Jerry. He had a quick smile and seldom cried unless he was picked up. Dad put a bed in the living room so he could be with the rest of the family. Carold wanted to be left alone on the bed and watch the other boys.

Jerry on the other hand loved life rough and with Donny. Jerry was happiest when he was in his stroller, handles removed, being pushed around the living room or the kitchen table by Donny. I went too slowly to suit him and Jerry loved speed. Carold enjoyed being talked to or read to. I loved to read to him.

Our home was a very sad place after the baby died. There were no more fast rides for Jerry. It was as if Mom was afraid something would happen to him. The laughter had gone from our home. I remember the day Dad picked us up at school and stopped at our mail box on the way home. Aunt Dora was waiting to talk to Dad.

At this time Dad worked the day shift at Allis Chalmers and got home in time to drive on south to our school and pick us up in bad weather. Now Mom wanted us picked up every day and she would worry until we got home. We walked most of the time because of the gasoline shortage but we rode to school with the neighbor kid's mom if she took her kids. But that was usually when they were late and we were already at school. Aunt Dora made it a habit to visit Mom during the day. In today's world the Doctors would call her condition depression and could give her medication for it. Back then there was very little done about it. Knowing Mom as I did I am not sure if she would have taken the medication or not, I just do not know.

The message Aunt Dora had for my Dad was, "You have to get her out of that house where her baby died. She needs new interests that will take her mind off her loss." I could see that Dad agreed with her.

A few weeks after their conversation Dad and Mom loaded our family into the car and went for a drive. I thought we were going to go visit Mom's parents, Mom and Dad Richards.

As we neared our grandparent's home we saw several things going on. We didn't turn into their drive. Uncle Ray and our cousin Ronny were in the front yard. Uncle Ray was Mom's youngest brother and raised hogs and he and Ronnie were gathering the mounds of acorns for the hogs. Ronny was the son of Moms youngest sister Vesta. Mom and Dad Richards had unofficially adopted Ronny after his parents divorced. As we drove past Uncle Ray waved at us, Dad honked the horn and Ronny looked dumb founded that we didn't stop. Donny laughed like crazy at the look on Ronny's face. Ronny and Danny were the same age.

We drove on south, then west and then south again past a school house on the corner. About a quarter of a mile down the road on the west side was a large two story home and Wilkerson's welding shop. The next homestead was on the east side of the road, at the end of a long drive where an elderly couple named Wolfe lived. We learned later this was where the telephone line stopped. There were two more homes on the west side of the road before entering the timberland and up and down some hills. We went past the house where Uncle Buck and Aunt Clara lived when I got hit in the face with the tarpaper roll disk a couple of years earlier. The house stood brooding, empty and dark under the old trees in the yard. My uncle's family had moved to the little town of Breckenridge. There was a little valley between the empty house and the house we were going to look at.

Finally we stopped at the next to last house on a mile long dead end road. The house was empty. There was a barn, brooder house and hog sheds south of the barn. We all walked about the house, to the barn, to the out buildings and finally to the top of a small hill where we could see trees at the end of an unplowed corn field. Dad said that where the trees were was also the river. Farm implements sat abandoned all over the place. Dad was quick to notice that gates hung on broken hinges and weeds grew everywhere. It appeared the previous owners had just walked off and left the place. We went back to the house and Mom started picking up junk and made a pile in the middle of the floor. She said in no uncertain terms this place was a mess! Dad checked the well pump and we all washed up, then Mom and Dad sat in the car talking while Donny and I "explored" some more.

Sometime later a man and woman arrived. There was a lot of serious talk going on so Donny and I were sent to play. I remember really liking this place. There was so much more room to run in than where we lived. The barn was about the same size as ours but we could tell there had been horses and cows here! We had no horses or cows so our "little kids" imagination went wild. And there was a big apple orchard across the road east of the house. The man came to our house a few times but Donny or I heard nothing more about the "new" home and we sort of forgot about it

Then one day Dad picked us up from school. The days were getting warm and sunny now so this was sort of unusual. When we got home Mom and the little boys had several boxes packed. She had taken down the curtains in some of the rooms washed them and they were drying on a line outdoors. Mom looked happier than she had for a long time. They announced to Donny and me that we were going to move. We weren't even going to finish the school term at our old school. Dad told us we were going to move to the place we looked at over by Mom and Dad Richards. The next few weekends they spent getting the house ready to move into. Mom continued to wash and iron curtains. She packed up household goods, pictures and things we didn't need at the time.

The decision to move prompted Dad to begin working in the #8 coal mine at Tovey with Mom's three brothers and two of her brothers–in–law, very much to the disappointment of Uncle Charlie. Dad was driving several miles to Springfield and a lot less to the mine where he worked second shift and could start farming, which was my parents dream. World War II gasoline shortage did not allow him to drive that much so he and Mom's brother Uncle Buck rode to work together, taking turns driving.

As soon as they could get the house livable to Mom's standards we moved in. Mom made a big trash fire in the barn lot just south of the house and burned the rubble the last owners left. She painted walls and woodwork starting in the kitchen first. Then one Saturday and Sunday Mom's brothers Uncle Buck, Uncle Charlie and Uncle George helped Mom and Dad move the remaining belongings into our new home. Mom continued to paint and clean, she and Dad papered the bed rooms and living room of our home. Donny and I never tired of exploring and dreaming of all the animals we would have. By night time we all were so tired we fell into bed. When Mom finished painting all the woodwork and floors, she started on the big summer kitchen, and porches. Dad worked at repairs on the outside like Mom worked inside. There was a lot of work to be done.

As soon as we moved into our new home Mom took us to our new school for just the short time till school was out. We lived a mile from our school which was named Star School. Donny and I were very happy and our new school was fun even if Donny and a boy named Alfred did dislike one another on sight.

To this day I am grateful our nearest neighboring family with someone like Donny lived more than three miles from us. That's still pretty close to have two, one-kid demolition crews.

It was a yearly ritual that as the weather became warm, Mom and Dad moved beds dressers and cabinets outside for a good cleaning or fresh coat of paint or varnish. Wood work was washed and stoves were blackened and setback for the summer. In our new home Dad repaired even the smallest things Mom found. She loved our home and she sang as she worked. She could beat rugs or wash quilts and sing to high heaven. When the spring cleaning was done she was ready to make garden and help put in farm crops or repair fences. Our home had no electricity or telephone and it was smaller than our old house, but we were all very happy.

There was an orchard with peach trees, a cherry tree, a grape harbor, apple trees and a plum thicket along a west fence row. Mom was thrilled with the orchard and walked among the trees in the evening. Dad and Mom had bought the farm which consisted of house, barn and outbuildings on twenty acres of land. Later on there was another twenty acres they would rent and then they began to buy. It was located in Christian County and became known to the family as "Christian Forty."

There was however a sad note. First, Uncle Ray had been drafted into the Army and was now stationed in Germany, where there were fierce battles going on. Mom listened to our battery operated radio every night for the news. Also it was a sad day for us to leave Aunt Dora she was a true family friend. Through tears Mom and Aunt Dora exchanged gifts. Mom gave her a large crocheted tablecloth and Aunt Dora not to be out done gave Mom several hens and a rooster. Donny looked pretty serious when she gave Mom a pair each of ducks and geese. This was the start of Moms poultry enterprise.

Uncle George brought us a young collie dog we named Frisky, and Mom welcomed him, she was certain he would make a good watch dog. Dad bought Uncle Rays hogs. Boy life was good!

Aunt Dora came to visit every couple of weeks and she would bring us eggs and cream until we got our own milk cow and the hens started laying eggs. Somehow it always happened to be baking day so Mom would send her home with baked goods. Aunt Dora, her mother and her brother loved Moms sweet rolls, noodles and bread.

For years Mom and Aunt Dora would go to South Fork cemetery just before Decoration Day later renamed Memorial Day, to clean and rake the graves of those who had passed on. They took a picnic lunch and worked and visited, it was a day for remembering.

Mom was most respectful of all the graves and she demanded the same from us. We were never allowed to run or yell or climb on the head stones. The families that allowed this behavior were looked down on as being unruly. Aunt Dora referred to them as ill-bred children. The cemetery was located in back of the South Fork church with tall old cedar trees along the drive. A timber was located on the south and west side and it was a quiet peaceful place. Many years later I took my own child with me as I did the same tasks that my Mom performed at the same graves. She always spent extra time at Carold's grave planting a pink Peony on his grave.

On one occasion Donny and I went to the back of the church to look in the basement windows. Mom had told us we had to be quiet as there were people of the church inside working. Quietly Donny and I tiptoed up to the window to see what it looked like in the basement. We had attended funerals at this church but that was all. As I stuck my head up close to the window I felt as though I had been hit with a baseball bat. I got stung right between the eyes by a hornet. Well, so much for quiet!

The sting hurt so badly and almost immediately my eyes became swollen shut. Mom and Aunt Dora took me around to the front door of the church where the ladies were working. Aunt Dora was a member of South Fork church and she knew where the baking soda was kept. Mom washed the sting area and made a poultice of the baking soda and my face began to feel better.

Many years later I would remember this remedy when my husband stepped out our door with our baby son and a bumble bee stung him in the face.

The beginning of our life on Christian Forty was a very promising venture. Immediately Mom got better, that's not to say we didn't find tears in her eyes when she rocked Jerry. She and Dad built a chicken pen for chickens, ducks and geese and her flock began to increase. Dad bought a milk cow and a team of horses. A bay mare named Molly that Donny claimed and a strawberry roan mare named Queen that I claimed. Dad plowed up an area north of the barn lot and driveway and we put in a large garden. We were beginning to be self-sufficient. Mom even had eggs and butter to give away when neighbor women came to call. That summer they cleaned and resurfaced the outdoor cave, or cellar. Dad built shelves all around the inside.

At Peabody Coal mine #8, Dad worked with Moms brothers, Buck, George, Jim, and brothers in law Frank and Teed. He could work in the mine on second shift and farm until time to go to work. Dad and Uncle Buck repaired the abandoned farm machinery. We were in seventh heaven. Dad put in a corn crop that amounted to about twenty acres but as we often heard Mom and Dad say, "it's a start." During grown up talk we had heard Dad and Uncle Buck say they knew when the mine tunnel went under the river because of the water running down the walls. Donny and I just knew they meant the river at the end of our place which was South Fork. I think it caused Donny to wonder if Dad knew some of the things he was up to.

∽∂◌∾

We had more freedom living on a dead end road. There was one more house past us where an elderly gentleman lived. However with Dad working nights, Donny had much more time to think of ways to get into trouble and time on his hands was not good and as the old saying goes, "idle hands are the devils play ground." This began a very happy time in our lives and for about six years my life was ideal.

We had limited radio (battery operated) usage, it was saved for evening programs and important news, we did not have electricity and people had to make their own entertainment. I sometimes wished Donny had not tried so hard. I am sure I would not have some of the scars on my face I now carry.

I was the eldest child Evelyn Maxine, overly tall for a girl, a tomboy, with long brown braids and resembled mom in height only not pretty like she was. Next came Donny, Donald Lavern he was small for his age and as wiry as whitleather. He had been very ill as a baby, and was close to death at least twice before the age of two. He had dark blond hair like Dad but Donny's hair never looked combed even after it had just been combed. Cow-licks on his head added character, or so Mom said. A whorl on the face of a horse is said by some horseman to be the sign of an unruly horse. A whorl is similar to a cowlick. At any rate Donny had two. One on the back of his head and one in the hair line over his right eye. Being fourteen months younger than I, certainly never stopped him from trying to badger me and every other kid in school into some of his hair-brained ideas. I don't believe the word "can't" was even in his vocabulary.

Third child in the family was Daniel Leroy, Danny, and at a very young age he had already proved to be a dare-devil. "If Donny can do it so can I", was his motto. He caused me several near heart attacks trying to keep him out of harm's way. He had dark curly hair like Mom, was of medium build, and strong for his age. He was sweet natured, and so loveable he could talk his way out of trouble, just like his hero Donny.

Fourth child was Jarold Ray, Jerry and he could melt an iceberg with his smile. He was a good baby as long as he could be with the family but he certainly was not a loner. He had dark blond hair like Donny and Dad but it was curly especially when it was wet.

⌇⌇

Our second term at school was started in the fall. Our first term was very short since we had moved here and started school in the spring. The school was located a mile north of our home and we walked to and from school of course. As in any new school there are kids you become good friends with and some you did not really care for.

Donny managed to find both. One of his best friends might just as well not have had a first name as far as Donny was concerned. He referred to the boy as the, or that "Beatty kid", or just plain "Beatty" these were terms of real friendship.

However, Donny and Alfred became enemies on sight. It was of small consequence that Alfred was the taller by about three inches or that he was heavier than Donny. They were worse than two Bantam roosters. I have often wondered what the teacher thought that first morning when Donny and Alfred glared at one another across the room. It seemed to be a very small room with those two in it. It became a constant worry as to when a fight would break out. Alfred's sister Helen and Sue (the Beaty kid's sister) and I were friends. Maybe it was our brothers that bonded our friendship, sort of like a tornado or other disaster brings folks closer to one another.

I loved each new school term. We saw the kids we hadn't seen much of since school was out for the summer. Mom wouldn't let us go as far from home as some of the kids lived. After the twin baby died she wanted us where she could see us or know where we were. I don't think she smothered us but she at least knew what direction we were from the house. By the time school started Mom had spent many long hours at her treadle sewing machine. She would move it out on the porch so she could be outside during the daylight hours. She ordered some of our clothes and household goods from the Sears Roebuck or Montgomery Ward catalogs.

She also would pick out certain patterns when Dad bought feed, the sacks came in printed material and Mom made shirts or pinafores for me out of them. She could take the more unworn parts such as the back of the legs of Dads pants and sew them into pants for us kids. She even used the faded worn parts to tear into strips then she braided them and sewed them together to make throw rugs. When she cut out a dress or shirts from new material she never threw away any scraps, instead she made quilt blocks and then a new quilt. I was tall and skinny so skirts and blouses were out for me. Mom made pinafores which I liked much better for dress up then I didn't always have someone telling me to put my shirttail in. Aunt Sina gave Mom dresses as she got too big for them. Mom could remake a dress until the only part that was recognized was the color or print of the material. Mom could do wonders with a sewing machine.

During the first part of the new school year at Star School Donny and Alfred fought with no real harm done. However their competitions became a problem for their sisters, when a fight started between them it meant Helen and I had to stop whatever we were doing and go try to stop the fight. As Donny's sister I had constant hopes that he and Alfred would learn to live in harmony or at the very least learn to ignore one another. I was always too embarrassed to ask Helen how she felt about our feuding brothers. Our school years at Star School were well remembered, sometimes in not such a good way.

Going to a country school the girls and boys all wore shirts and jeans or overalls. (However a few years later when the school district consolidated the rural schools the girls had to wear dresses. That was a different ball game. I had to stop being a tom-boy and act like a lady and Mom meant every word she said.) The first day of school we had new jeans and shirts that had only been worn once or twice before for some occasion. We had new boxes of crayolas, new tablets with just one page written on and unsharpened pencils. The school always smelled of new paint and freshly oiled floors. Everything was new and fresh, however some things never changed, namely Donny and Alfred.

I always looked forward to the first day of the new school term. Donny on the other hand had to hear a threat from Dad before he finally realized summer was over. It took almost all the will power Mom had to get Donny on the road to school let alone her prayers that he would get there with everything she started him out with. Our third term at Star School began with a bang. Since Donny was the only pupil in the second grade the teacher put him in the same grade with Helen, Sue, Don B. and me, third grade.

That was a big mistake as the promotion went to his head. For some reason he believed that he was smarter than the rest of the class, and set out to prove it. This notion made for some very interesting class sessions. What was taught and what Donny heard was sometimes as different as daylight and dark. There were even times that we caught the teacher or her assistant (an eighth grade student) smiling at Donny's interpretations of the instruction. And of course he never tired of telling me that he was smart and I was a "dumb ole girl." No one ever knew where he got this mind set as he certainly was not taught this at home.

This school session started where the last left off. Donny and I would see the Funderburk kids as we rode our horse past their house on our way north to our grandparent's house. Funderburk's lived south of our grandparents. We all would speak and wave as we passed but the boys had no chance to argue.

Helen, Sue and I became friends and that friendship remained until I moved to Indiana when I was fifteen years old. On the other hand Donny and Alfred remained like two Bantam roosters circling each other. They circled and they circled and they glared and they would postulate each trying to intimidate the other. They managed to interrupt my favorite time at school which was music and when the teacher read to us. I can remember sitting in my seat at school, Donny glaring at Alfred and Alfred glaring at Donny. I looked over at Helen hoping she didn't see how embarrassed I was because my stupid brother wanted to fight! Years later I would discover that she was as embarrassed as I. But this was just the beginning! I finally got enough nerve many years later at a High School reunion to ask her about our brothers fighting. Her answer was "I just wanted to choke him!" Amen! Those two were mortal enemies from day one. Silly ole me, why had I thought this year would be different?

It made no difference if they had identical objects, swings, ball and bat, jump rope, each thought the other one had the best. This attitude would make for a very interesting school year. The boys continued to act the fool. At some point the boys in the school decided to make a club house underneath the school house. In the brick foundation in the back of the school they found a few loose bricks which they quietly worked at to remove to gain entrance under the building. They continued to work solid bricks loose. This would be a prolonged job, as they reset the loose bricks at the last recess of the day.

Of course no girls were allowed near the back of the school house. Donny even tried to keep me from looking at their handiwork as we passed by on our way home. I am not certain as to what happened but when the battle was over there appeared to be a story. As bricks were being removed one or the other bumped the opposite persons hand with a brick. Each boy said the other one started the fight.

Well Katy-bar-the-door, now it became an all-out war. In the melee they had each smashed the other ones hand with a brick. Such screaming and squalling, it sounded terrible. This incident eventually blew over and the boys continued to work at removing bricks. Finally they hacked away until they could crawl under the school house.

Now our teacher had ears like an owl. She could hear a whisper before you spoke. So it didn't take long for her to figure out something was going on. She rang the bell but of course the boys under the school house didn't hear it. Before we could take our seats there was an eruption with such a racket it made a cat fight sound real tame. There was a banging on the floor that I hated to think if it was heads, hands, feet or even bricks. The teacher disappeared out the side door in a flash and her next idea wasn't the greatest ever. She demanded the culprits repair the wall. If the situation was bad when they fought with fists imagine them having bricks in their hands again. The end result was Alfred hit Donny on the leg and Donny smashed Alfred's hand. I believe one of the school board members did the repairs because the hole just sort of disappeared and the two boys went on to different competitions.

⌒♫⌒

During World War II the schools and any boys or girls organizations, scouts and 4-H kids were asked to search and collect milkweed pods. The fluffy white inside the seed pods was used to make life jackets for the Navy. Milkweed contents replaced something called kapok which grew on trees in the East Indies, but was lost to the Japanese during the war. Uncle Ray was in Germany so all his nieces and nephews joined in the effort to collect the milkweed pods. Mom cut burlap sacks in half, stitched the bottoms and tied the tops together leaving a small opening for us to put the pods through. At first we gathered the pods on foot and then we started riding our roan mare Queen to collect pods faster and easier. Dad showed us how to hang the bags over our horse's withers or flank. Which we did and off we went to gather pods.

We would ride back in the fields around us and collect hundreds of the pods. We were sure our pods went right to Uncle Ray, no stop in between even though he was in the Army not the Navy. Of course there was a competition for each family to see who could gather the most pods. We emptied our bags into the bags hanging on the back fence at school to dry unless it looked like rain then someone would come to our school and take them away. I don't know where they were taken or who took them. Donny and I just had fun collecting the pods on horseback. We thought we were helping win the war. And we just sure we were helping Uncle Ray.

❧◦❧

All the kids in our school carried their lunch to school. None of us lived close enough to go home for lunch. Some of the kids had square bright colored boxes others had Roy Rogers or Gene Autrey or Hopalong Cassady on their lunch boxes. Some of the kids and Donny and I carried half gallon lard buckets.

Our boxes weren't pretty but the other kids gathered around to try to trade their lunch for ours. They had sandwiches with store bought bread and lunchmeat and a store bought cake. Mom packed sandwiches made of pot roast, ham or chicken on homemade bread or fried chicken and deviled eggs in cool weather. Small glass jars contained fruit, cake or a piece of pie. I didn't trade. We ate breakfast early after chores in the morning, so by lunch time I was hungry and sure did not want to trade away my lunch. Sometimes Mom would put a surprise in our lunches. Dad was fond of fudge and Mom made the best. This was a lunch box treat.

Sometimes holidays were celebrated when Mom made a cake for the whole school. Once one of the kids saw Mom drive up to the school and jumped up shouting "your Mom is here and I'll bet she's got cake." By the time Mom entered the cloak room the kids were waiting for her. She never tarried, just said a few words to our teacher and left. I never minded carrying the cake pan home at night, it was always empty. Chocolate was the school favorite.

When we got home from school Mom had thick slices of homemade bread, fresh butter and her jam or jelly with peanut butter or a sprinkling of cinnamon sugar. Our favorite programs before chores in warm weather were Roy Rogers and his horse Trigger, the Lone Ranger and Tonto with their horses Silver and Scout, Gene Autry and Champ. Then off we went to see what changes the world-our world had made while we were at school. In the winter we did chores as soon as we got home.

We did all our home work at school but we had to practice our letters and numbers after chores and supper. Donny and I had tablets at home that we had to work in at night. Mom had to see improvement or you had to do more pages. I think my mother was a frustrated teacher. We ate apple slices while we worked and Mom washed dishes. Then we all moved into the living room and listened to the radio. My folks didn't believe in idle hands so we shelled seed corn or popcorn. Mom crocheted every spare moment she had. I have seen a sleeping baby in her arms as she worked magic with her needle. She always had mending of clothes or socks and used a small glass egg in the toe of the sock to make a smooth seam. Mom listened to Stella Dallas, The Thin Man, Green Hornet, and Ma Perkins and as the mystery got scary we moved closer to Mom's chair. Bed time was eight sharp, no excuses. Mom sometimes stayed up till Dad got home around midnight from work. It was not unusual to smell cooking and fresh coffee or hear them talking in the kitchen. It was very reassuring to a kid.

Donny lived with an awful lot of pain when he was growing up, most of it his own making. Everything he associated with turned to ruin, so why did I let him talk me into his schemes? Because he had a gift for making the most ridiculous seem plausible.

July and August was the usual time for the county to oil the roads. The black slick hot tar was sprayed on the road after the road had been graded and leveled. It took several days for the oil to soak in and become solid. We children were told to stay away from the road. This admonition would have been OK except the oil truck backed into our drive to turn around. It was a magnet for Donny.

During this time Dad kept the horses off the road. It was hard enough to get the black glue like stuff from the car, and doubly hard to clean the horses feet with the gooey stuff on them. With much intense study Donny figured out that if he was careful he could step in the oil then in the dust and sit down for it to dry. He surmised that a good thick coat of oil on the bottoms of his feet and he wouldn't have to wear shoes when school started. He just knew the kids at school would wish they had thought of this plan. He did hate new shoes. He tried to tell me that I was really missing out on a good thing, the oil would be gone pretty soon and I wouldn't have shoes like he did. He worked hard to get several coats on his feet, and sacrificed much, after all he couldn't play while his "shoes" dried. He spent most of the afternoon in the shade of the lilac bush at the end of the yard. He was so proud of his effort that when Mom came to check on us he informed her that he wouldn't need school shoes.

Mom was horrified when she saw the black soles of Donny's feet. She knew the tar could cause the skin to blister and to peel off. He was so disappointed when she made him sit with the bottoms of his feet soaking in coal oil. Then she scrubbed and washed until all the oil was off his feet.

One should not take advantage of, nor enjoy another person's ill fate but I sure did enjoy the time he had to sit there and also had to be quiet. He had tried very hard to explain to Mom why he "needed" the "oil shoes". She wasn't buying any of it. For once one of his hair-brained ideas did not include me as a guinea pig.

New shoes were always a part of returning to school each fall. We usually had some type of wound or a stubbed toe on our feet which made trying on or wearing new shoes an ordeal. Donny and I took our shoes off when we walked home. We loved going bare foot.

∽∂ᄋᄾ

When I was nine years old Mom decided to take me to get a permanent in my hair for my birthday and the new school term. I think she was trying to exorcise her tomboy daughter. Perhaps she had a Shirley Temple transformation in mind. I had no idea whatsoever what I was in for, and did not know how much of my long hair would be cut off.

It took forever to get my thick hair on rollers. It had been cut to collar length, no more long braids. The machine was a monster of a thing and the curlers were so heavy. The curlers got hot and stunk to high heaven. Mom kept telling me I was going to be pretty. I thought that was wishful thinking or some type of hopeful miracle.

Finally I was "done". The curlers were removed, my hair washed and dried and combed and then I was turned around so I could see myself. I had no idea who the person in the mirror was. I looked like I had been struck by lightning! My hair frizzed all over my head and the beautician kept patting and pushing at it in an effort to make it lie down. Mom was speechless and I started to bawl, no simpering cry for me-I bawled.

We went straight home and Donny came racing out of the house, stopped in front of me and started to laugh. For that I tried to pinch his silly little head off.

Mom fought my hair every morning until it grew out enough she could pull it back and fastened it tight with a rubber band and ribbon. It took a long time for my hair to grow out enough to have braids again. It was years before I had my hair cut off again. Mom trimmed my hair herself and cut my bangs. It gave new meaning to her saying "and this too shall pass."

I liked school even in winter when we walked to school. For me a good school day was great when Donny and Alfred weren't fighting. I never minded doing the chores that all the kids took turns doing even though when it was your turn you had to get to school early. We carried water from the outdoor pump to fill the water cooler inside the cloak room where each child had a tin cup to drink from. We took turns dusting the blackboard and then cleaning the erasers on the back step. The older boys carried in coal and carried out the ashes. Everyone put the ashes in their driveways, so the school drive was always in good shape.

Music time was a favorite for all of us. We learned the song "Don't Fence Me In" of course Donny and Alfred had to try to outdo one another until they got THE LOOK from the teacher. I liked it when she taught us to sing harmony.

Right up there with music were the days when she read to us. All grades one through eight would gather in a semicircle sitting on the floor. My favorite book was the story of Old Mother West Wind and her children the Merry Little Breezes. She instilled a love of music, although I did not have a good voice, and of reading in me that would last lifelong.

After a long day at school and chores it seemed Donny and I still had lots of unused energy and King of the Hill was one of our favorite games. One of the really great things on our farm was the cave or root cellar located just to the northwest of the summer kitchen. In today's modern times my parent's hub of operation would be called an office. It was a large underground cave built out away from the house. It was covered with several inches of dirt and grass grew over the mound. The walls were lined ceiling to floor with shelves for Moms canning. A small table and chair sat near the back where Mom graded and candled the eggs and this was where she put the cream separator together after she had washed it in the house.

Near the right wall was the cream separator, a tall shiny machine with a great stainless steel bowl on the top. Shelves near the right side of the entrance held the farm books, livestock records and a steel box held the important papers and family records. Mom was deathly afraid of fire so the cellar was the logical place to keep important papers. Surprisingly it was cool and dry down there in summer yet it did not freeze in winter.

My folks kept calendars everywhere, in the kitchen family and friend's names magically appeared written next to a day of the month. There were calendars in the horse and cow barns which contained names of each animal and mysterious dates and words written next to them. There was a calendar in the corn crib with the word HOGS written at the top. Mom even kept a calendar for her chickens, ducks and geese. She knew which females of each species were likely to end up on the Sunday dinner table. Periodically the calendar pages were taken to the cellar for entry into Moms books. My parents were conscience of time, both days and hours.

The cellar had the familiar smell of lye soap and Mom kept it as clean as her kitchen which was always scrubbed clean at the end of the day. Soon after we moved to Christian Forty Donny and I discovered the cellar was an ideal place to play King of The Hill. Since there were just the two of us we had to improvise. The rules were simple, we both started on top of the cellar, each ran in the opposite direction around the house and back to the top of the cellar. Whoever got to the top and could keep the other one from climbing up was the winner.

At the north east corner of the house grew a Bridal Wreath bush. We found that by going behind the bush we could cut off a few feet of ground and perhaps get the edge on the other person. I cannot imagine how it must have sounded inside the house when we slammed into the building, but it did not take Mom very long to get outside and put a stop to it.

Everything went fine for a while until we both got the idea to sneak between the house and Mom's prized Bridal Wreath bush being careful not to hit the house. We met head on at the corner. My being taller than Donny did not have any advantage in this case. My two front teeth just scraped the top of his head. If we had been smart we would have each nursed our wounds in silence, but instead we both screamed the Banshee scream.

Mom came running to take care of the latest problem. When she found we were not badly hurt and how we got hurt, she cut a little switch and the two of us forgot our pushed in teeth and scraped head.

❧❧❧

I had few real dolls in my life time. And I did not play with any of them. One really belonged to Mom and was made of glass and very dainty. Another one was a beautiful baby doll with real blonde hair, eyelashes and beautiful eyes that went to sleep. And such a sweet lovely smile. I never played with the doll, just sat and looked at her, she was so beautiful. I often wished I had looked like her. I had seen baby and toddler pictures of myself - I was no doll.

I can't remember her name for sure but Jane comes to mind; she was mine such a short time. My doll sat on a shelf in the closet all day and I would take her down in the evening after chores and supper to look at her. I would not let the boys touch her.

One day when Danny and Jerry were about five and three years old they took my doll down from the shelf - just to look at her I am sure. Her two tiny front teeth fascinated them and when I had her out they would want to see how her eyes opened and closed and to look at her teeth. Jerry was positive she could bite with her two tiny white teeth.

While I was at school their fascination for her teeth caused them to want to touch them, they ended up pushing the teeth back into her head. They must have been panic stricken to see what had happened. Not only would they have me angry at them, but Mom had also told them they must not touch her. In their young minds they must have thought they had to fix her; they broke her, they must fix her. They used something to try to pry the teeth back in place and broke off part of her lip.

When I got home she was lying face down on my bed. I can remember the absolute horror when I picked her up and looked at her wide (real wide) toothless grin. I screamed for Mom and both little boys flung themselves at me crying, saying they didn't mean to hurt her. No one could have looked at those two pitiful little faces and been angry for long.

The doll was relegated back to her shelf. I could see her every time I went into the closet, but she had lost her fascination for me. I didn't even mind that my hair was straight and dark, while she had beautiful blond curls.

I don't think the little boys ever peeked inside that closet again. Finally I just gave her to them to play with. Jerry carried her by the arm, leg or hair.

My second doll was something of a cross between a clown and a doll. It was a sturdy, toss-me-where-you-will doll. I don't remember how I became the owner. By then we had horses that I could ride, so I never paid much attention to the doll.

By leaving this doll out it also became open season for the little boys. At any given time one could see her being carried by a leg or an arm across the yard. She was left out in the rain, which did not do anything for her looks but then she was a very durable doll. The boys soon found other things of interest. Mom was burning some trash one evening, as folks did then and asked me if I wanted to keep the doll. By this time it was hard to tell what the little critter was supposed to be. I had no interest in her so we tossed her to the fire. That was the end of my doll phase of life. As far as I was concerned no doll could compete with horses.

3

Chores

Spring time was always hectic and every project a family affair. Even the two little boys "helped" when Jerry was old enough to follow. The garden was no exception. In the fall Dad would plow and prepare the ground for next year. Mom always planted peas when it was still too cold to be outside for any time. It would be too cold for chores but not too cold to play.

Good Friday was the day to plant potatoes. So Mom and Dad and all four of us kids would head to the north garden where most of that garden was planted in potatoes. With six of us and always lots of company it took several bushels of potatoes per year.

With seed potatoes, knives, buckets and kids the folks were ready to plant. Dad used our strawberry roan horse Queen to lay off the rows wide enough to use the cultivator on, so all we had to do was plant and cover. Our parents taught us how to lay the cut side down with the eyes of the potato up. Mom and Dad planted two rows each while Donny and I planted one on either side of our parents. We had to be careful how we handled the cut potatoes so we didn't knock the eyes off.

We all thought we were doing very well until we got to the end and looked back over our work. There was Danny and Jerry with their buckets picking the potatoes UP! Mom said that when she got back to them, Danny was pretty angry that the four of us had gotten so far ahead of him and Jerry doing their "thing". It was as if he thought he was supposed to pick up as fast as we planted.

The folks took pride in our home and the garden, which Mom considered mostly her domain. Dad moved the potato garden towards the road I think it was to show it off. The large vegetable garden was straight south of the summer kitchen through the yard gate. Also afternoons the large shade trees put the garden in shade for a while. Weeds had no chance with Mom. During the summer she canned everything we couldn't use. Her shelves in the cellar were always full to overflowing. She would take last year's canning off the shelf to make room for the present years produce. She always kept her kitchen shelves well stocked.

Late afternoons would find Mom snapping or shelling beans or shelling peas sitting outside in the cool of the porch. Those were afternoons she told us stories about when she was a girl. She talked a lot about her horse Cricket. Sometimes I think Mom liked horses as well as she did people. And she was definitely a people person. I think she liked working in the garden almost as much as driving or riding the horses. While she worked she sang, mostly gospel songs. I am not sure where Mom learned the songs since we did not attend church nor did our grandparents on either side of the family. Mom quoted passages from the Bible and took their meaning quite literally. Sometimes she could be found reading the Bible at night while she waited up for Dad to come home from the coal mine. She had a good strong singing voice, which I did not inherit, not by a stone's throw close.

Dad rented a meadow that was connected to the apple orchard across the road from our home. He pastured the young Tennessee Jersey heifers in the meadow until they had their calves.

After the cow had her calf we took the mother and baby to the barn where we tried to domesticate them. They were always as wild as March Hare when we got them. Dad often warned us kids that these heifers had seen very few people and not to try to pet them. Of course Donny was sure that did not mean him. He believed he was the exception to all rules. The folks made every effort to have safe animals for us kids to work with, and as on any farm Dad had to train or break the animals, be it to work or milk.

Our work team was Queen and Molly and they did not get rattled at much of anything. Dad could park the wagon in such a way as to isolate the cow from the calf. Dad or Mom, as either were efficient at the chore and worked as a team, would jump from the wagon, put the calf into the wagon bed and be back on the wagon seat by the time the cow got around to where she had last seen her calf. If the calf was a few hours old it sometimes took some doing to get cow and calf into a small pen and catch the calf for the trip home.

Usually the calf would bawl up a storm and the cow would follow along behind the wagon. As with all generalities there were exceptions. The exception this time was the calf didn't bawl, it just reclined in the straw in the bed of the wagon and seemed to enjoy the ride.

The two little boys always rode up in the box seat of the wagon with Mom and Dad, while Donny and I rode in the back. This particular time the cow kept bawling and staying where her calf had been. She couldn't seem to understand that her baby had gone off and left her. Finally Dad stopped the wagon in hopes the calf would call to its mother. It didn't make a sound, but the cow sensing the calf was in the wagon soon caught up with us. When the wagon started to move the cow just stayed where she was bawling for her baby, we did this several times.

Donny, one to never leave well enough alone, started yelling for me to hold the calf up so the cow could see it. Of course "dumb ole girl" that I was I did just that as the cow reached the back end of the wagon. NOW the calf bawls, the cow lunged with her two front feet in the wagon almost on top of me.

I was shaking and my teeth were chattering. I yelled for Mom (too late now) but the horses had stepped into a trot and the cow fell back to the ground. I yelled at Donny, asking him "why did you tell me to do that?" His answer was, "aw I knew she couldn't really get in the wagon." Well, you could have fooled me! I wanted to pinch his silly little head off!

❦

During the haying season Mom cooked for all the men in the hay crew when they were at our place. There was one farm wife that paid Mom to take her turn. The hay crew never seemed to mind the extra mile to and from our place when Mom cooked dinner. Sometimes there would be as many as five or six extra men to feed. The hay crew went from farm to farm baling hay. Dad and an elderly neighbor shared the hay from his field and Dad paid the crew and Mom cooked their meal as payment for our hay. This meant Mom would be up cooking from early morning till noon baking breads, preparing vegetables, making noodles, meats, salads and desserts. It seemed to me there was an unspoken and sometimes spoken rivalry among the neighborhood women as to who set the best table. I can't speak for the other women but my Mother set a very fine table. No expensive china or silver but excellent food served on a brilliantly white table cloth.

For hay crews or when family came to our house which was almost every Sunday, she cooked in the summer kitchen. The kitchen cooled off pretty fast with the north and south windows open. Some of the men preferred to eat at a table in the yard and return to the kitchen for refills. My job was to keep iced tea glasses full. It seemed the crew would be there for dinner although they baled later in the day.

On this particular day Jerry was sick with a fever that he was plagued with for many years. It wasn't a high fever but enough to make any little guy cranky. At times like this I would sit on the porch and rock him until he went to sleep. Sometimes it worked and sometimes it didn't. Danny who was about five years old at the time seemed at a loss when Donny wasn't around. Donny was in the hay field with Dad and the men for the first load then he would stay at the house and pump the water tanks full so when the men brought horses in there would be water for them.

I heard Mom in the kitchen talking to Danny. After a while Danny came out doing an exaggerated high stepping tippy-toe walk, a very good imitation of Donny. When he went past me rocking Jerry he put his finger to his lips in a hush motion. Silly ole me I thought he was motioning that he didn't want to wake Jerry.

As soon as he was off the porch he started to run around the front of the house, his little bare feet making little fat dust puffs as he ran. About the time he was out of sight Mom called from the kitchen. Going to the living room window she scolded Danny, he had "tasted" the icing on one side of her cake. No wonder he made little dust puffs as he quickly moved elsewhere, if she had caught him in the kitchen she more than likely would have "dusted" the seat of his pants.

One of Mom's cardinal rules were clean hands. We always had to wash our hands when we came in from outdoors. Anytime we had been to the barn, henhouse or garden or anywhere in between we had to wash our hands at the enameled wash basin that sat on a table in the corner of the dog run. The dog run (and I have no idea why it was called that since Mom would not allow the dog in) was a wide open connection between the house and the summer kitchen with screened doors on each side. It was equipped with a heavy soap dish, the inevitable lye soap, clean towels and a mirror hanging on the wall, a water bucket and a dipper. Just inside the kitchen door stood another wash stand with an almost identical bucket, wash basin and lye soap. Woe to the kid who missed either of these washing stands. It was Mom's rule in her kitchen to wash your hands twice. Just one time of Mom taking you by the ear back to which ever wash stand you missed and you never forgot again, only twice satisfied Mom.

The summer kitchen was about one and a half times larger than the main kitchen in the house. This was where Mom did laundry in the winter time, where the winter meat was prepared when butchering and in the summer it was always busy with canning and preserving the winter's food supply. Every Sunday some of Mom's family, brothers, sisters and their family gathered at our house for dinner. Mom did all the cooking, the sisters in law stating they could not do as well as Mom. I don't think they ever tried very hard. But Mom was pretty particular about her meals so it was just as well. This summer kitchen was where

Mom was preparing dinner for the hay crew but she had the deserts on the table in the main house.

After the first load of hay was unloaded and the men were heading back to the field Mom took Jerry to rock and sent me to put out clean towels at the wash basin and at a bench under the big tree in the yard. The hay makers would wash up out there. Then I was to go to the garden, probably for green onions.

When I took the towels out to the wash bench Donny was pumping water into the big watering tank for the horses. I went to the garden then stopped at the dog run and washed up. I stepped to the door to throw out the pan of dirty water – just as Donny ran past the door! The water hit him full in the face.

He didn't make too much of it for which I was grateful and I forgot all about the incident. I went to the front porch where Mom was now rocking Jerry and she in turn gave the child to me as she returned to the kitchen. Finally Jerry went to sleep about the time the team came into sight. As the team got even with the house, Donny came hurling himself in high gear from the back yard yelling at the top of his lungs that I had thrown dirty water all over him. Dad gave me a frown and a sour look. Not good! Jerry woke up and started to cry, Mom came to the door to tell Donny to be quiet, but by then he was out of sight racing down the yard to beat the horses to the drive.

❧◦❧

Early morning, before sunup was the second favorite time of day for me, first was sunset. Autumn was my favorite season, I knew winter was coming but I didn't care I loved autumn. The two little boys began waking up and the animals were always glad to see us. By the time the two of us older children were called to get up, Mom had biscuits ready to bake in the wood/coal stove. While I was getting dressed I kept an eye on Danny and Jerry who might or might not be still sleeping. If they were awake they would be in full speed ahead to get somewhere.

Mom would go to the barn and start feeding the horses. Dad would have the first two or three head of milk cows in the barn and started the milking. Mom would come back with the bucket of milk and take it to the cellar. Usually she put the milk separator together as soon as she had it washed. It was a very precise chore to put the cone shaped disks on the center cone. It took several minutes to put it together. The milk and cream were separated and each came out one of the two spouts; the milk into a bucket and the cream into a cream can that sat on a small table Dad had built to hold two cans.

The buckets of separated milk were carried to the pig pen and poured into a huge fifty-five gallon drum and was mixed with ground corn, cobs and all, and ground oats. The mixture was called swill. This is not a fond memory of mine. I hated to have to mess with it, but it was a farm chore and that meant getting it done. The hogs loved it but in the summer the smell was awful when it fermented.

Mom would check on Donny to see why he had not gone to the barn yet with the milk buckets. This was a daily routine. By then Donny would have managed to "accidentally" wake Danny and Jerry and I would get them dressed. Danny would race to keep up with Donny. For a time Jerry was happy to play in the kitchen, while I set the breakfast table. All too soon he became old enough to try to keep up with Donny and Danny. Dad would bring in the next bucket and they would get that milk started in the separator. Dad and I would return to the barn where Donny, Dad and I finished the milking. Mom went back to the kitchen to finish breakfast and pack school lunches.

My position in the milking barn was just inside the barn door. Donny would be two cows behind me and Dad was at the back of the barn. I always suspected that Dad positioned himself where he did so he could keep an eye on the whole barn. Donny loved to try to spray milk into the mouths of the barn cats. Dad would know Donny was up to something when one or both of the little boys giggled. Dad would stop whistling the tune Red River Valley (about the only song I ever heard Dad sing or whistle) and say "Donald Lavern". The barn would get quiet for a while then Dad would squirt a stream of milk at a cat's mouth and that would send gales of laughter from all the boys. Being at the front of the barn I would miss the action. It never failed to make me smile just to hear the others laughing.

When the six to eight cows (depending on how many had calves at their side) were milked and the milk taken care of we all headed to the back porch to clean up for breakfast. Jerry would be at the door to greet us and get into the fray. Breakfast would be biscuits bacon sausage or ham, gravy and eggs or oatmeal.

Once breakfast was over Donny and I slopped the hogs, while Dad started harnessing horses to go to the field in summer, or in winter he would cut wood and haul it to the house. With the hogs taken care of, and it was never too soon for me, Donny and I would turn the cows out to pasture leaving bawling calves behind.

～❧～

One morning Dad sent Donny to the hayloft to throw down a bale of hay. Danny of course followed Donny running as fast as they could go. It wasn't long before the bale of hay fell to the ground. I was to put the hay in the hay bunk for the calves to learn to eat and the cows would finish later. Donny stood in the hayloft door surveying his domain. I soon heard the boys talking in low anxious voices. Then Danny began to cry, and Donny started to yell for Dad, Danny had followed Donny up into the loft and was afraid to come down. I was terrified that the little guy would fall, and I started yelling for him to stay back. Dad came running to the barn from hitching a team and down the hallway to where the ruckus was. He climbed the ladder to the top and helped Danny to get one leg over the edge. Then he and Danny started back down the ladder. Danny felt safe with Dads arms on either side as he was given time for each little hand to grip and release coming down. Dad kept telling him to not look down, to look at the top of the barn as they were climbing down.

Both boys were pretty grim as Dad warned them not to do this again. He did not have to tell Danny twice not to climb up to the loft.

Danny found other things that were just about as much fun. Of course just following Donny was an adventure in itself.

The days of summer were true paradise for me. The mornings were cool and fresh and by afternoon you could feel the heat on bare feet and taste the dusty sun. Late afternoon would feel used up in time for the sun to set and start to cool off. The sound of tree frogs and locust would make a promise that tomorrow would be as good as today had been. We went to sleep to the sounds of owls, whippoorwills and night hawks calling from the edge of the timber. Closer to the house mocking birds and cat birds would call and I almost always went to sleep before they quit calling. Those were jewel like days in the life of farm kids.

✌◎✍

I have always believed that hogs should go straight from baby pigs to a "growing place" away from me. I do not like grown hogs. Especially sows with baby pigs, they are so picky about who picks up their babies. During the time that Dad was raising hogs it was an accepted practice to feed swill to the hogs. A mixture of ground corn and oats from the elevator mixed with water and milk and fed to the shoats. Since we milked several cows, the cream was separated and sold and the left over milk was a boon to this hog feed mixture.

We had to be very quiet when we mixed the swill with a long handled wooden paddle in the fifty-five gallon drums. Any sound would bring the hogs racing and squealing to the feed trough. The idea was to pour the swill into the troughs before the hogs reached the trough. They loved to wallow in a mud pond down in their pasture that was fenced from the garden and fruit trees and duck pond. If you got caught in the pen with them not only did you run the chance of being trampled but they were muddy, and if you got knocked down, you were a muddy mess!

We had to take turns going into the pen and filling the lower end of the long trough full to start with, hoping the hogs would start there!

As the hogs ate we could then pour more swill down a shoot into the trough.

On the day in question Donny and I had bickered and quarreled all day. It was my turn to fill the troughs which numbered three at this particular time. The hogs were large and about ready for market. It took several buckets full of swill to get the end of the troughs full. I was pouring a bucket full into one of the troughs when Donny "accidentally" banged the empty bucket a few times against the metal drum.

Before I could empty the last bucket the hogs burst from the pond, muddy bodies racing straight at me! I emptied the bucket as fast as I could and ran for the fence. I didn't make it, a big mud covered hog skidded up to the trough pinning me next to the fence. I was covered with mud from my waist down! My bare feet had been tromped, and I was mad as a hornet. Donny got on his horse and made his-self scarce while I was taking a bath and getting rid of the stinking mud on my jeans. I spent the next hour trying to find Donny, I wanted to pinch his silly head off!

One thing that could be counted on for certain was that if a hog had "lost" the ring in its nose or was just oblivious to pain it would find a spot in the fence where it could get its nose under the wire and by hook or crook it would get out. So it was that we had a large black and white belted hog that made it a life's exercise to get out at least once a week. It was most likely to get out into the yard. When we heard the old hens set up a racket we were sure the hog was out.

Mom would call Donny and me and our dog Frisky to come help get the hog out of the yard, into the barn lot and through the gate and back into the hog pen. All of this without letting any other hogs out, and hope he didn't get out again before Dad could close up the hole where he got out. I think if Dad had been home when this hog got his afternoon urge to wander the results would have culminated sooner.

The day in question was hot, muggy and threatening to storm. Mom, Donny, Frisky and I had worked the hog along the fence slowly about a dozen times. Each time the hog got to the open barn lot gate it would dash past and we would have to start all over to slowly drive him back towards the gate, again. The hog had no fear of us. I think it just enjoyed the attention.

Danny and Jerry had been placed in the little wagon up near the summer kitchen and told to stay there. When Mom or Dad used a stern or severe tone to tell us something we knew to listen up, even the little guys. We always had fair warnings but if we chose to ignore Mom and Dad we had to pay the consequences.

It seemed to me we had worked with this hog for hours to no avail and the storm clouds were getting darker and the heat was oppressive. The hog would amble along the fence then run past the gate and back out into the yard. But the last time when it got to the gate Donny yelled "get him Frisky." The dog had a position between Mom and Donny, and shot out after the hog and as it turned to run Frisky grabbed it by the ear. The momentum of his body threw the hog off balance and it landed on its side. The dog held on growling every time the hog tried to move.

We all stood around trying to catch our breath until Mom called to Frisky and slowly he backed off growling. The hog got slowly to its feet and with Frisky alongside the hog meekly went through the yard gate and then the hog gate. Mom had thrown ear corn to the hogs at the south fence so they were no problem. Frisky escorted the hog into the hog lot and as a final act of discipline nipped it on the leg. The hog squealed and went off to rest if it was as tired as we were.

We had no idea where Frisky had learned to subdue hogs, since he was about a year old when we got him, but he had the maneuver down pat. We would learn later that he could throw a large cow by grabbing her nose and throwing his body to one side.

After we had the chores done and were at supper as the storm raged out side Mom asked Donny how he knew that Frisky could stop the hog. Donny was never one to hide his light under a basket said, "cause I taught him to do that and he is a good cow dog too "better'n some dumb ole girl." To our knowledge at that time he had not thrown a cow. That got him a rebuke from Mom and an apology to me.

No one seemed to wonder how or when Donny had trained Frisky. I think the dog was just smart and his herding instinct kicked in. Thereafter when a hog got out it was a pretty simple job to get it back in. Frisky was a constant companion with us and sometimes if he had to choose he would stay with Danny and Jerry especially if Donny and I were on the horses. Dad didn't want him out running the county so we tried to make him go back if he followed us. His job was to look after the two little guys.

<hr/>

Folks who live in the country and are responsible for livestock are always aware of the weather. Storms can wreak havoc with crops and buildings and cause bodily harm to humans and animals. Summer storms are seldom ignored by farm families. One such storm boiled up with black thunder heads and closer to the ground a yellowish color that indicated hail. Dad sent me to ride Queen down to the pasture to start the milk cows to the barn lot. If we were quick enough and the storm wasn't moving too fast we could get the chores done before the storm reached its peak.

Queen was a rock solid horse and was pretty cow smart. She could crowd a cow into moving along towards the barn. I was driving the cows along the fence when the wind and blinding rain caught up with us. I drove the cows into the barn lot and turned the horse around to ride out of the pen as Dad was ready to close the gate. As Queen turned around she touched her hip to the electric fence on the south side of the pen. Several things happened in a sequence of events. The ground, the horse and I was wet, the fence was hot. The horse got an electric shock which ran through her and then to me.

The horse screamed, I screamed, the cows already nervous over the storm began to run in circles. Dad was shouting for me to jump off before she got into the fence again. I jumped off right into a puddle of mud and water. When I looked up the cows were in a semi-circle looking at me. Queen had come to a halt at the gate. Dad slipped the bridle off Queen and turned her into the pasture as the second wave of the storm came through, this time with hail, lightening and wind.

I was soaking wet but since it was still raining hard I didn't change clothes until the chores were done. I would long remember the electric fence incident and so did Queen. She seldom got close to the fence unless Dad made her when she was working.

❧ ❦

Baking day at our home was very special, large loaves of bread with light brown crusts, and always big wonderful cinnamon rolls came from Mom's oven. Farm folks did not go to town for a loaf of bread, and since we were pretty self-sufficient otherwise, baking her own bread just became a regular chore for Mom. I always knew the day she was making bread. When I came in from chores, into the kitchen there would be that good yeasty smell. She would have already had the bread made and set to rise by chore time. There is nothing like the smell of rising bread and perking coffee to set ones taste buds working overtime.

All day at school I would think about that hot buttered bread, it was a weakness of mine. As soon as school was out we would say good-bye and head home. Just as soon as we got on the road home Donny would say, "I am going to beat you home and get the "heels" from all the bread!" Tormenting me was a weakness of his. For those unaware the heel is the end crust of the loaf of bread. Well the race was on, if the term race can be used. Donny could run like a scared rabbit, while I ran more like a sleepy turtle. In comparison to Donny I was just running in place. I was tall, skinny and should have outrun him but I just could not run fast.

In my heart I knew he was not going to get all the crusts, for one thing Mom did not cut into a second loaf of bread until the first one was finished. However on baking day she would cut both ends off and have them ready for us when we got home from school. But that didn't make any difference, just the sight of Donny's back racing ahead of me and gaining distance was enough to set my temper to boil. That dumb cow-lick on the back of his head stood up in a little sprig as he raced bare foot for home.

When we reached home, out of breath and worn out from running most of the mile home, sure enough there was plenty of hot bread, fresh made butter and homemade jam. To make things great Mom and the two little boys would sit down and eat with us, before we all went out to do the evening chores, Dad was at work, so the chores were ours to do in the evening. Danny tried to mimic everything Donny did, and Jerry thought Donny and Danny were ever so funny; Mom really had to watch the two of them. Donny knew he could rile me anytime by saying "I am going to beat you home and get all the heels."

⚜

Our big summer kitchen was the most actively used of the two kitchens. The kitchen was used often for many things that kept any mess out of the main house. It consisted of a long room and as wide as the main house. Mom cooked and served large meals out there. Almost every Sunday mostly in the summer time would find some of Mom's five brothers and their families at our home. Mom was a stickler for clean. Woe to the kid that tracked mud into the house. After a good scolding they could just get bucket and cloth and really clean up their mess.

The kitchen was equipped with a big black iron cooking stove with space for six or seven large pans at one time. The front of the stove was hottest and as the surface went to the right there was less heat. Cooked food was placed to the far right to keep it hot. There was a large warming oven across the top and a water reservoir for keeping water hot. Hot dish water was always ready. The stove in the main house was less than half the size of the one in the summer kitchen. That's another thing that was never explained to my satisfaction. If this was a summer kitchen why did we work out there almost all winter?

There was a long table that when I was a kid it appeared to go on forever. It would seat twelve to fourteen adults and babies in highchairs easily. There was a kids table in the corner, close enough for the adults to hush us when we got too loud. The windows along both sides of the room were four feet high above the floor and all along the north and south walls. Dad had built long oak sideboards into the walls that were sanded and varnished until they gleamed. This was where Mom stored the dishes, pots and pans and the heavy silverware, that wasn't made of silver. I didn't understand that misnomer either.

Summertime was always busy and Mom spent many of her afternoons out in the summer kitchen canning, making jelly or baking. My folks raised a large garden and always had a very big potato garden. As the potatoes were dug there would be some nicked by the plow, Mom canned these or they were put in vegetable soup that she canned. Also she canned fruit from the orchard. She placed the fresh jars of canning on the sideboard and then she and Dad would fill a wooden box and between the two of them carry the canned jars to the cave. It never froze down there and was ideal storage for the root crops. Mom's canning was a source of pride with Dad and he would take visiting family to see the work she had done.

Each year at berry season she would hitch the horses onto the wagon, load us kids into the wagon and we would pick the berries in season; strawberries, black berries, dew berries, wild raspberries, gooseberries, elderberries and wild cherry. I much preferred to pick berries from horseback since I was so sure that there were snakes lying in wait for me. Donny would rattle the bushes and tell me he saw a snake, I knew better but it made me nervous. Danny and Jerry would play in the wagon Mom had parked in the shade and she, Donny and I would pick berries. When we got our bucket full or it got heavy we poured the berries into a tub in the wagon. By the time we were finished Danny and Jerry had "sampled" the berries and had berry stains around their mouths and on their hands.

I liked picking wild strawberries best. There were no thorns and I had no problems with Donny. He was allergic to poison ivy and I wasn't so I could pick carefully and not have to be told to hurry up.

The first picking I would eat about as many as I picked then I didn't want any more off the vine. They were very good on shortcake with thick cream or whipped cream. When there appeared to be enough for Mom to make jam she and I picked together. Those were wonderful days when I had her to myself.

The gooseberries grew in a fence row and Donny and I picked them. Dad could pick blackberries, dewberries, and wild raspberries while most folks were thinking about it. He loved any kind of berry pie and Mom usually canned several half gallon jars. Dad seldom wanted cake but he sure loved pies. When you put together a cold morning hot biscuits, fresh butter and any jelly or jam it makes all the work of gathering worthwhile. The gooseberries were an adult delicacy as most kids didn't like the tartness of them and rhubarb wasn't a favorite of mine.

Mom's sisters and sisters-in-law admired her pantry with row after row of canned vegetables, fruits, jams, jellies and pickles but to my knowledge none of them except Mom's sister Sina did any canning. Uncle Charlie would ask Mom to bake him a pie once in a while but they didn't pick anything.

Out in the kitchen was a rocking chair and Mom would rock the little boys until they went to sleep then she would put them down on a pallet on the floor or in their bed in the house. She always wanted to know exactly where her kids were or as close to knowing as possible.

When the Maytag washer was not in use it was stored in the back corner covered up. Mondays were laundry day at our house and that was done in the summer kitchen. Mom and Dad carried water from the well that was heated on the big stove in the laundry tubs. Donny and I carried in the benches from the side of the house. The benches were heavy and used for a multitude of activities, but not for play you could get into trouble pretty quick for romping on Mom's laundry benches. Dad had screwed eye hooks into the walls about a foot from the ceiling and tied clothesline rope to them so that there were four lines the length of the long room. Mom hung the wet clothes in this room and the heat from the stove dried them. Some of the larger pieces were still hung outside and would freeze dry in winter. The ropes were removed when we had company. Everything was hung outside in summer.

Mom did her ironing as the clothes dried. She heated the irons on the stove. The big table was used to fold clothes on. On wash day there was always a kettle of vegetable soup or soup beans cooking while she did the laundry. The oven would have a special desert called Lazy Day Pie. Another misnomer, it was a cake batter with fruit poured over the top. The batter would rise through the fruit forming a golden crust and Mom served thick cream over the warm "pie". It was a favorite of mine and I still make it for my family.

One summer afternoon Mom was doing her laundry in the summer kitchen, we had a gasoline Maytag washer. They were notorious for being difficult to start. It had run out of gasoline during dinner time. Dad filled the gas tank, started the machine and left for work.

A short time later Mom returned to her laundry and went past the window to gather dry clothes. She said her heart stopped beating – there was smoke coming out the window. Mom was so afraid of a house fire and she panicked. She screamed for Donny and me and sent us to Mr. and Mrs. Wolfe's home to call the fire truck. Our horses were in the pasture southwest of us and she said we didn't have time to get them. She told us to run as fast as we could to have Mrs. Wolfe call the fire department. We did.

After the fire truck was called Mr. Wolfe took us home. Danny and Jerry were still asleep in the main house in their after dinner nap. Mom had pumped the well dry, which happened often in dry weather. In her panic she forgotten that Dad had hauled up two fifty-five gallon barrels of water from a well located at the bottom of a hill north of our drive and they were at the hog pen in the back yard. She had carried buckets of water two at a time up the hill from that well and had the fire under control. She had also used water from the horse tank and laundry rinse water.

When Donny and I got back home Mom was so tired and her face was beet red from exhaustion but she had the fire out. It was quite some time before the Edinburg fire truck arrived. They had to go to the river to fill the water tank. Mr. Wolfe thought that was poor planning, saying the whole house could have burned down. With the arrival of the fire truck there were neighbors who followed it to our place. A fire truck in the neighborhood was cause for alarm.

All the commotion awakened Danny and Jerry and Danny had hundreds of questions I could not answer. We sat on the bench under the big tree in the side yard with Mom and stayed out of the way. Donny on the other hand was everywhere giving his opinion which no one seemed to hear. Mr. Wilkerson a neighbor who ran a welding shop surmised the washing machine had back fired causing a spark to ignite drops of gasoline. It took Dad some time to fix the burned kitchen.

Large cooking kettles hung on the wall behind the stove. The laundry tubs and butchering kettles were hung in the smokehouse. They were brought out in the late fall during butchering time. Mom's Dad and four of her brothers would come to our place to butcher calves and hogs for all the families. Since my uncles lived in town Dad raised the stock then his brothers in law would buy whatever their family needed for the winter. Each time they butchered it would be two hogs and one steer. Everyone but our family had electricity. Each family took their own meat home for storage in their freezer or to a locker plant in Springfield or Taylorville. My grandparents had a smoke house that some of the family used for their smoked meat also some of the hams were salt cured. I did not like salt cured meat.

The big kettles were used to render lard, cook the meat for head cheese and mincemeat and to mix the sausage before Mom fried it. Dad Richards would not allow anyone but Mom and himself to season and make sausage. Mom's brothers helped Dad with the actual killing and processing the meat. The summer kitchen became a meat processing room. None of Moms sisters in law were ever present during the butchering. However when Mom cooked dinners with the butchered meat all the wives were present.

The sausage was fried and then packed into stone jars and the hot grease poured over it and sealed. Then the men carried the jars to the cellar for storage. When Mom wanted sausage she dug up a layer, lard and all and placed the meat in a baking pan in the oven. She removed the lard as it melted to fry eggs and make gravy or to fry potatoes.

I liked to do homework or play in the summer kitchen it was such a cozy active room. However I really got into trouble once for standing Jerry on the table. Mom went into a panic and snatched him up into her arms. She scolded me telling me I was never to do that again. Her sister Emma had been crippled when two of her sisters were playing with her, letting her walk across a table to each other. She walked off the side and crippled her foot. At that time, more than a century ago, foot surgery was not done except as an absolute emergency.

4

Donny and More

One evening and it must have been a Saturday or Sunday because Dad was home, Dad called Donny and me to do the milking. Both of us had been playing in the front yard. On the second call I started running towards the barn, I would have to slow down long enough to open and go through the barn lot gate. Always the competitor Donny went around the north side of the house and intended to duck under the barbed wire gap across the corner of the north barn lot. Running at top speed Donny didn't duck under the wire low enough and the wire caught him across the face just above his eyes. The Banshee scream split the air and Dad and Mom and I took a short cut to the north side of the house.

The barbs of the fence cut into Donny's forehead and blood ran down his face and onto his shirt. He tried to cover his face to stop the blood. What I remember most is that blood ran between his fingers, I don't do blood very well so while Dad and Mom bandaged Donny up Danny Jerry and I sat on the bench beneath the tree by the well.

Danny had seen dead animals and there had been lots of blood so his question to me was, "is Donny gonna get dead?" Jerry started crying and then Danny took up the cry and they both clung to me crying. Mom rescued me from the crying little boys and took them into the house. Dad called me to help with the milking.

When we got back to the house from finishing the milking and Mom had separated the cream Donny was on the sofa in the living room enjoying the attention from Danny and Jerry, his head swathed in bandages. He was explaining to his audience how he was suspended on the barbed wire. He made it sound like a real adventure and Danny and Jerry hung on every word.

A few days later when the bandages had been removed he stood on tip toes to see his scars in the mirror and declared that they looked good. Somehow he equated scars to macho and a scar looked good? Oh well whatever.

∽◦∾

Donny liked to think of himself as a loner, preferring to "do it myself", but somehow he always needed "just a hand" for a minute. That hand was usually mine and then I was in real trouble. He was always thinking, thinking of a "better" way to do even the simple every day, time proven chore. He was sure he did not need help for his "inventions" which was his name for everything he built or did. However he always had someone else to try out his ideas on.

He could think up and abandon ideas faster than the average kid could think, I believe this was the reason he was misunderstood. Even his teachers had the vague idea that he "wasn't playing with a full deck". When he did settle on an idea for an invention he would go about the project like he was killing snakes. Sometimes he could visualize himself as being someone else and would even refer to himself as such and such a person. He liked to tinker but wasn't much for chores or anything that vaguely resembled work. With a little luck he might just invent something worthwhile someday. At least he had me convinced as he would delight in telling me his way was better faster and easier. When we were finished his way was almost always slower and more difficult.

One time Dad brought a wagon load of feed from town and parked it out near the feed lot gate. Part of the load was for the hogs and the rest was to be mixed for the cattle. Our job was to put a five gallon bucket in our little handy-dandy Radio Flyer wagon, each one of us used a large coffee can and filled the bucket about two-thirds full. We would then pull the wagon to the barn and the two of us could easily lift and empty the bucket into the feed storage bin. I've often wondered why Dad didn't park the wagon closer to the barn and I imagine the mischief factor was involved. I think his intention was for the job to take us longer and therefore keep us out of mischief.

After a couple of trips Donny decided he had a plan to do the job faster. While I loaded the bucket and took the feed to the barn, Donny was building his "miracle plan". I worked for what seemed like hours alone. All the while I could hear the pounding and banging of the miracle plan. Finally it was finished and he called me to see. His invention was the most unbearably ugliest sled I had ever seen. The runners were crooked and no two boards on the top were the same length. He had fastened a rope on the front to pull it with.

We put the bucket on the "miracle sled" filled it up and started to pull it to the barn. I don't think I ever tugged and pulled and struggled so hard in my life. The rope made my hands sore and just about the time we got to the barn one of the runners broke off and the feed spilled onto the ground. Naturally it was my fault because the runner was on my side.

Mom came out to see what had caused the racket and fight and after helping clean up the feed she told Donny he was to use the wagon and bring the feed to the barn, one bucket at a time, as I had. He was not happy, being the consummate inventor he was certain his time could be spent so much better than doing mundane chores. He was certain that he had more feed to haul than I had. Once this chore was completed he was off to bigger and better things.

⌒∂⌒

During this time Dad had rented a pasture from a neighbor about a half mile north of us. He had three or four horses he was breaking and therefore we were short of pasture. Dad pastured the older team of

Queen and Molly at the neighbors place during the night. During the week Dad checked on the horses on his way home from work.

When we got to the pasture Dad and Mom sternly warned us to be careful around the horses because of horse flies. When the horse flies landed on the horses all they wanted to do was get rid of them and it usually meant bucking and kicking. Donny evidently didn't hear or else ignored the warning because he crawled through the barbed wire fence and ran straight for Molly's broad rear end.

Killing horse flies was one of his favorite pastimes. Just as he got to Molly's back end she kicked out. She kicked him in the lower part of his body, hard enough to send him flying backward under the barbed wire fence. I was never convinced that it was an accident, I didn't like Molly. He was badly injured. Dad and Mom got all of us back in the car and took Donny to the Doctor in Edinburg. Since the horses weren't shod it wasn't as bad as it could have been. The Doctor talked to Mom and Dad but I don't know what was said. The only thing Mom told me was that they would have to watch Donny closely for several days and wait to see if there was internal damage. Donny had to stay in bed for a long time and although I never saw it Mom said Donny's lower body was one large bruise.

As time passed Donny was out of bed more each day until he began to be more like himself. It was very lonely without him while he was bedfast. At last the day arrived when he wanted to ride his horse. Mom didn't think it was such a good idea but told us to ride very close to home where she could see us. He appeared to not have any problems so we were out of the woods with that accident.

♋

With some kids there are those who just seem to draw trouble to themselves. These are kids that parents hate to see leave the house. They knew with certainty that there will be blood before the day ended. Donny was one of these kids. Of course the attitude of the kid has a lot to do with how many scars are collected. Donny was a person who thought of himself as invincible, and continued through life to try to prove it. There was no job, problem or situation that was too difficult too big or the lack of knowledge for Donny not to attempt. He may have never seen the problem, or situation before but he knew all about it. Mom and Dad kept the clean milk buckets and cream separator in the cave. One evening Mom sent Donny to get the milk buckets. She had not had time to put the cream separator together. The cone shaped discs had to be placed on a spindle in exact order. The numbers were imprinted on each disc. There was only one way to get it right. Not so for Donny. Being the helpful little scout that he was he put it together and even had a couple of the cones left over. Since we kids were not supposed to touch the discs I am not sure how he accomplished this feat.

When Donny took the buckets to the barn he told Mom she didn't have to worry about the cream separator that he had put it together and if she needed more "of them round things" there was a spare on the shelf. Even I could see that Mom was not impressed but Donny went about his business as if all was hunky-dory. I think this is the first time I became aware of the term "pick your battles." I think she knew there would be another one soon enough.

✧

Some kids are naturally accident prone. These are the kids that set out to make things right with the world. One of Donny's favorite past times in the winter was to knock icicles from the eaves of the sheds, he would even go into the duck/goose pen to "kill" icicles. During the gardening season my folks put the hoes and rakes on top of the chicken house. The edges of the tools were hooked over the crown of the building. The reasoning being the little ones could not get to them and they were near the garden. Unfortunately I was not considered a little one and when the hoes or rakes were on the roof of the chicken house I was happy.

We had an early freezing rain before the tools had been stored in the shed for the winter. Icicles had formed on the eaves on the north side of the buildings. As we started to the barn to do the milking Donny was in one of his "what can I do for excitement" modes. As we passed the chicken house, he picked up a long stick with the grand adornments of Danny's stick-horse. Giving me his milk bucket, he proceeded to drag the stick-horse back and forth along the eaves, breaking off the little icicles. Danny would not have been happy to see his horse up in the air. After all he had left it tied the night before with a hand full of grass at its nose and that was where he expected it to be when he started his day.

I went on to the barn, Mom seldom called more than twice to do chores and I was sure she had already made the second call. She was driving the cows into the holding pen to be milked. As I went through the yard gate I heard Donny's Banshee scream. Mom came running and I held the gate open for her as she raced to her squalling offspring.

Donny had knocked the hoe loose from its perch on the chicken house roof and as he went about his business of ridding the world of dreaded icicles the hoe fell, hitting him in the back of the head.

Mom rushed him into the house, calling Dad. Dad had only been in bed a few hours. It is surprising how a screaming kid can just shake the sleep right out of a person. By the time I got the gates closed and got to the house, Jerry was crying and Mom and Dad were bandaging Donny's head. They put Donny to bed, Mom took care of Jerry, and Dad and I milked the cows. By the time we came in for breakfast Donny was up admiring his bandage. Over a huge bowl of oatmeal Donny asked Mom if she thought he would have a "nice scar?" I don't remember what her answer was but I remember Mom gazing heavenward with a pleading look on her face.

✍∂❀✑

Dad bought us a second hand bicycle from somewhere and for a while Donny and I took turns riding and learning to ride. I was learning and Donny who knew everything already knew how to ride. For a while we had fun just riding the bike without much fuss. Then the chain began slipping and Dad told us to park it until he could fix it. Donny, one to never leave well enough alone decided he could "fix it."

That afternoon after Dad went to work Donny proceeded to "work on the chain." After a period of tinkering he declared the bike fixed. He told me to ride it while he ran alongside to watch the chain and boast of his handiwork. We started off and I went north, because I was not very good at turning sharp or even semi sharp turns and I did not want to go down the steep south hill. Everything was fine until we came to the first little hill. I tried to stop but started going faster than I wanted to go and when I put on the brakes the pedal suddenly spun backwards. No brakes! I was going faster and faster and Donny running alongside was shouting orders at me, mostly "fool don't wreck the bike or you are dead!"

The next thing I knew I was off the road heading into a steep blackberry briar and young sumac filled ditch. Everything became a blur until I finally reached the bottom. Unwinding myself from the tangle of bicycle and briars I looked up to see Donny come flying into the ditch. Silly ole me I thought he was coming to help me. He was mad as an old wet hen and he was screaming at me. The jest of his tirade was that I was just a dumb ole girl, too stupid to ride a bicycle!

We managed to get the bicycle out of the ditch and back on the road. What a sorry sight that was. The handle bars were set at a 45% angle, the fender carrier hung by one support and there was a small limb sticking through the rear wheel. The front wheel had spokes bent in several places. Half carrying, half pulling Donny started for home with his beloved bicycle. I was heartbroken that I had wrecked his prized possession but he would hear no declaration of an apology.

In the next few days Dad managed to repair the damage I had done and also fixed the chain, Donny was happy as a lark in spring time. Danny, Jerry and I sat at the edge of the yard and watched Donny race up and down the road, his cow lick standing up on the back of his head. Somehow the bike riding did not appeal to me anymore, besides we had horses and however in the world could a bicycle compare to a horse?

～✦～

While summer with long days and no school were special winter was also fun. Dad got us a sled that would carry Danny Jerry and me and we would ride for hours on a windless day. Donny rode the sled alone head first down the hill! The road in front of the house and a hill south in the pasture was ideal.

Donny got bored easily and one of his inventive moods took over. Mom thought the little guys had been outside long enough so I took them in doors. Then Donny and I headed for the big hill behind the barn. We had a wooden kitchen chair in the barn that Mom had once used to tie Jerry in to keep him safe while we milked, if he could not be in the empty corn crib she had swept and cleaned, where she could see him. By the time I got to the barn, I was pulling the sled, I found Donny taking the legs off the wooden chair to make a sled. Never mind that we had a perfectly good sled.

When he was finished taking the legs off he took the rest of the chair out to the hill, he sat cross legged on the seat facing the chair back. He thought that it would be fun to glide over the snow downhill. I watched him go down the hill a few times and it really did look like fun. Finally he got tired and let me try it out. It looked so simple I was sure I could do it.

Donny told me I could go easier if I went down on the south side of the hill. He had been going down on the west side. I wasn't at all sure about this since the slope was longer and ended at the fence. I hesitated and Donny called me a sissy. That put the bail on the bucket. I sat down crossed legged on the seat, and took hold of the chair back and lunged myself forward as I had seen Donny do. I didn't go anywhere! Donny came to my rescue placing his hands on my back he gave me a shove AND a twirl. The chair began to spin over the crusted snow. All I can remember is seeing the world in a whirl of blurring snow and blue sky as the chair began to spin faster and faster over the packed snow. Around and around I spun becoming dizzy and disoriented.

Suddenly the chair hit the pasture fence sending me flying off into a snow bank. Dizzily I tried to pick myself up and there stood Donny at the top of the hill laughing like a fool. He quit laughing when he saw his sled in pieces. Groggily I watched Donny assess the damage to his chair-sled. He didn't even help me out of the snow drift, just went off muttering to himself something about dumb ole girls. With a nail or two and some baling wire he was soon flying down the hill again. This time I wasn't even tempted to want to ride I was not feeling adventurous. He sort of made himself scarce for quite a while. But fool that I was, I forgave him and tried out more of his silly inventions.

∽∾

Donny's next winter time crime was a sled made from an old green and white enameled Quaker State Motor oil sign. The top of the sign was rounded and had two holes in the top from which the sign hung in a frame in front of the local gas station. When the station went out of business the owner gave Dad three or four of the signs. One of the signs had the top bent upward. Donny fastened a pull rope on it and we pulled the two little boys around the yard. We were careful with the little guys because if they got hurt or started crying it was certain to bring Mother Wrath down on us two older ones.

At some point Mom thought the little guys had been outside long enough and took them into the house. Donny's imagination took over and we headed to the steep hill in the pasture. I stood back while Donny got on the motor oil sign/sled and lurched himself to a start down the hill. The "sled" went faster and faster and Donny began pulling on the guide ropes. Suddenly the sled began to spin out of control and instead of making the curve away from the fence the sled slammed into the heavy woven wire fence. The momentum of the sled hitting the fence was like a sling shot. Donny went into "my" snow bank and the sled continued on down the hill bouncing off the fence.

Donny sat chest deep in snow with his stocking cap down over his face. I laughed until I was too weak to run in case there was an angry brother attack. Suddenly I wondered if I looked that funny going downhill on a chair seat sled.

I watched as Donny dusted himself off, collected his sled and came trudging back up the hill. As he went past me he gave me a side glance that said "don't you dare laugh" I didn't, I wasn't such a dumb ole girl after all. I knew when to keep my mouth shut at least sometimes. In later years I wondered why Donny didn't think to hitch a pig or calf to his sled inventions. Since he appeared to have a death wish for racing, it should have appealed to him. Just didn't think of it I guess.

❧

The evening chores were done by Mom and us kids and there was not as much to do at night as there was in the morning. During the summer it seemed there was never enough time to get chores and play done before dark. We did not have electricity and Mom had a great fear of fire. I think for the times my folks were pretty tolerant of us kids, but they did expect us to do as we were told as soon as we were told to do it. When we were called to do chores if we did not respond and our folks called again using our middle name we had better drop everything and run.

Mom had called Donny for the second time. I was at the barn when I heard the Banshee scream. Mom told me to stay with the little ones as she ran to see about Donny. We had been playing horse shoes when Mom called. When I left Donny kept on pitching the horse shoes. Instead of putting the shoes near the stake, he threw them up in the air and then walked under one as it came down! The horse shoe hit him in the back of the head. His new scar was about an inch from the hoe scar.

❧

Why would any kid in their right mind want a one wheel "car"? Of course we are talking about Donny here. The four of us were very lucky to have a Radio Flyer wagon. Dad fastened a round piece of broom handle to the wagon tongue to form a T and I tied a rope to each end of the stick. I would then pull Danny and Jerry in the wagon. I was the "horse" and the little boys took turns "driving". Mom taught the boys to be gentle with their horse. I enjoyed playing horse and would pull the kids around the yard until I got tired. The stick on the handle also made it easier when Donny and I had to use the wagon for chores.

Then came the day when Donny decided to take one of the wheels off the wagon and invent a one wheel "car". He used two old plaster wall slats that he drilled holes about two inches from the ends. He then drove a bolt through one slat, the wheel and through the second slat. Thus far he had a V with a wheel at the narrow end. Next he nailed a cross bar at the wide end and nailed several old buttons to it for his radio and various inventive gadgets. Next he nailed on the stick shift. He took his car out to the road to the south and down a hill. Being at the end of a dead end road had many advantages and playing in the road was one of them. Of course Danny Jerry and I followed to see how this new wonder would work.

Donny raced down the hill as he described it "at the speed of light" with his cow lick standing straight up. He was so busy having fun he couldn't hear me ask for a turn, it is hard to get the attention of the speed of light. After four or five trips down the hill and one would think he would have seen the hole in the road, however the speed of light has little time for such mundane things. He ran his car into a small hole in the road oil. Donny was catapulted heels over breakfast and continued to roll down the hill. His car was in shambles, sticks really. Parts and pieces lay scattered everywhere. Suddenly the air split with the Banshee scream! He had driven a splinter into his hand.

Mom came running and told me to get those little boys in the yard, and went on to Donny. Helping him to the house she told me to get "that junk out of the road." Donny forgot his hand long enough to look up at her horrified at the word junk.

There was a lot of screeching and yells from the house and finally Donny emerged with a bandage on his hand. Of course he couldn't milk a cow or do chores but he managed to sit on his milking stool and explain what went wrong with his car and how he could fix it. Mom listened for a while then said in a voice that made us all listen up. "Donald Lavern you will put that wheel back on the wagon and put those sticks back in the wood pile, do you understand me?" Donny was quick to answer, "Yes Mom." That was the last of the "car" episode of course not the end of inventions.

⁓◌⁓

Ever notice how little kids all have imaginary friends or super powerful human ones? Many years later a member of my married family told me he had a bear for a friend when he was little and they ate bananas together, however he was the one that got sick. One thing they all have in common is the friend is always a constant companion. An extra place must be set at the table, a spot on a chair or a sofa is saved. Danny would put the vegetables he did not like on "Juneys" plate. I haven't the foggiest idea where the name Juney came from but a special friend needs a special name I guess. At any rate when the vegetables didn't disappear from Juneys plate, Danny had to eat them. I noticed there was never a problem with pies, cakes or any desert.

Now with Donny the story was unusual, his friend was a living breathing hero for one summer named Don Beaty. Of course when you have a "real" friend you call them by their last name, as Donny was so fond of telling me. The best ones have just one name, Superman, Batman and of course Beaty.

The Beaty family lived east of the school house and I heard a lot about Beaty that summer. He could jump, run and throw a ball farther than I could. He could catch more and bigger fish than I could although I never fished in my life. He could ride a horse faster than I could. The Beaty family did not own horses and no one was allowed to ride our horses, so how Donny knew this I am unaware. But Donny knew this to be a fact. In truth we never played with the Beaty kids away from school. We would have had to walk almost two miles to their home and Mom wouldn't allow us to go that far, unless we were sent on an errand to our grandparent's home riding Queen. And if we got off Queen we couldn't get back on without help.

Also Beaty could hit a baseball farther than I could, but of all the things Beaty could do better than I could, he still wasn't as good at any of them as Donny was. Donny was forever expanding and exalting Beaty's attributes but quick to mention he could do them better. Mom and Dad were always reminding us that it was wrongful to brag, but that didn't cut butter with Donny.

Then came the day Donny had a chance to show off in front of Beaty. One of the chores on our small farm that the whole family looked forward to was when we went to town to pick up the feed. A few days before Dad would take a load of corn to the elevator to be ground with oats for feed for the cows and hogs. When it was ready our family would take the wagon with side boards that were shoulder high on me and go to town to get the sacked up feed. Dad would put a couple bales of hay along the sides of the wagon for Donny, Danny, Jerry and me to sit on.

Mom and Dad sat on the seat up front talking and laughing, they knew we were pretty safe in the back. We were supposed to stay seated while the wagon was moving, but of course Donny seldom did. He would hook his arms over the sideboard and dangle his feet until he got tired or Mom saw him and made him sit down.

On this trip to town Donny was again dangling by his elbows when he saw Beaty. Beaty and his brother George were on the west side of their Dad's barn. I knew by the look in Donny's eyes he was going to do something, foolish. It wasn't that I was so smart for a girl, just that when he got that look it meant he was going to do something he was pretty sure Dad and Mom was not going to like. And he was usually right.

As our wagon drew near the Beaty farm Donny kept saying "I see Beaty, I see Beaty." I didn't think it was any big deal so I went back to reading. Things got un-naturally quiet, Jerry stopped asking me to read to him or asking what the pictures were or why. Danny stopped laughing at his hero Donny. I looked up to see Donny climbing over the tailgate of the wagon! I just stared. One of our parents rules were you never got on or off a moving vehicle until it stopped.

I gave my beloved book to Jerry to keep him seated, I was desperate. Danny by now was standing up on the bale of hay trying to see his hero who was out of sight. I got Danny by the arm and jerked him into seated position and started quietly to go try to help Donny back into the wagon. If Donny had gotten into trouble we might all have to sit out this visit to town in the wagon! And there would be no ice cream cones. Also did I mention that Mom and Dad would not tolerate tattle tales?

About this same time the horses moved into a trot. I lost my balance and fell flat on my behind. Looking up at the tailgate all I could see was Donny's white fingers dug into the wood. Many years later when I became a mother, I learned that extreme quiet means mischief where kids are concerned. At any rate whether it was the silence or her sixth sense, Mom turned around. What she saw were white knuckles gripping the tailgate, urgently she said, Donny, get back in this wagon." Donny heard none of it he was still trying to get Beaty's attention with "hey Beaty look at me, look Beaty what I am doing – hey Beaty." Again, and more urgently, Mom called, "Donny, get back in this wagon." All this time I could hear this exaggerated whisper, "hey Beaty look at me, hey Beaty."

"Donald, get back in this wagon, now. Evelyn, help him get back in the wagon." I peeked over the tailgate and there he clung, sun bleached blond head bobbing back and forth with that dumb cow lick sticking straight up, his feet swinging to and fro. This time the ultimate sound came from Mom, "Donald Lavern get in this wagon RIGHT NOW!" The use of one's first and middle names was cause for fast action. Mom and Dad were trying so hard not to have to stop the wagon and discipline an unruly child in front of the neighbors.

Donny dug his bare toes into the edge of the wagon bed and hoisted himself up on the tailgate and there he hung, too tired to help himself. I couldn't help giving a hard tug on the little fool. He fell into the wagon with a thump, got himself upright and sat on the bale of hay spitting and sputtering like wet dynamite. He was so humiliated to have his sister haul him in like a dumb fish. All the while Danny gazed at Donny in sheer adoration and wonder.

The funny thing about the whole episode was that when I looked over at the Beaty house as we passed, I did not see a single soul outside. I can only imagine that Beaty and his brother George had their own escapade going that they were more than likely not wanting their parents to know about.

Later on the way home, as we passed the Beaty farm "Beaty" was throwing ear corn to the hogs. He waved as we passed and of course Donny was again hanging by his elbows, feet planted on a sack of ground feed, his scrawny little toes dug in. He waved back ever so nonchalantly. A few minutes later, he off handedly mentioned that if Beaty had been helping him back into the wagon he could have "just yanked me right in, of course I could have got back in all by myself," he pronounced loudly, with his dumb cow-lick-standing-straight-up.

~∂∞~

I am certain the world would be a richer, safer place if someone could manage to get inside the head of a ten year old boy. In the span of time we lived on Christian Forty which was seven years Donny got into more trouble alone than the rest of us did together. Donny had a penchant for wanting to live in a tree. The big old sprawling tree in the front yard was his part time breakfast to bedtime home. One of the tree limbs grew out to one side and then turned up. Dad nailed some gunny sacks on the tree for a saddle and made us some stirrups, and he nailed on a rope for reins. When we were little we stood in our wagon or on a box to get on our "tree horse". When Donny and I outgrew our tree horse Danny and Jerry took it over. I helped Danny and Jerry to pretend to ride a horse. Donny and I had real horses to ride. Donny spent some time telling the little guys all about riding a horse. The little boys spent many long periods of time on their tree horse. Donny gravitated to his tree home. He could scale the tree almost to the top while I was thinking about it. I was never fond of heights.

About this time Mom was teaching me some of the finer points of being a home maker, crocheting being one of them. I would rather have been riding a horse.

When it was hot Dad did not want us riding the horses, so I was being taught something useful, and Donny was on his tree perch, a limb that grew about eight feet or so above the ground. Mom and I heard Danny say to Donny, "I am gonna tell." Now tattling was a pretty last resort at our house, as my folks did not respond to a tattle tale as a tattler wished. Mom and I went out onto the front porch and there stood the two little guys looking up into the tree.

Perched on a limb, several feet above our heads, sat Donny. He was barefooted (as usual) but in his hand was a large butcher knife. He had not heard Mom come outside as he was in Gene Autry mode singing to the high heavens. As we watched dumbfounded, he proceeded to trim his toenails! He was all absorbed in his task. Mom motioned me to get the two little boys into the house. I did not have to be told twice. Even Danny went quietly. We watched silently from the doorway.

Moms voice was extremely low and calm, as she said "Donald Lavern, I want you to drop that butcher knife to the ground."

Donny jumped as if he had been struck by lightning. He lost his balance and started to fall! In trying to turn loose of the knife and get a hand full of tree limb, he managed to cut his knee cap. He screamed the Banshee scream and bled like a stuck hog. When he got down from his perch, blood was running down his leg.

A neighbor lady named Eadie and her daughter Joanne who lived just south of us had recently moved into her grandfather's house was going by in her car and saw all the commotion. Jerry had a habit of crying when anyone else did, so of course he set up a howl. Mom and Eadie determined that stitches were needed to close the wound. They wrapped a bandage around Donny's knee and set off to the doctor.

I stayed home and took care of the little boys while Donny was loaded into the neighbor's car and they took him to the doctor in town, five miles away. Joanne stayed with me and the little boys. Once Donny was gone Jerry turned to Joanne with the biggest, brightest smile I ever saw. I am certain that if I had been left alone he would have cried all the time Mom was gone.

Of course when Donny got home he assured us he had BIG stitches under the bandage. This episode kept him from chores for a while. A couple of weeks later Donny took his own stitches out one evening while Mom and I were doing the chores. When we came to the house he proclaimed that he had a nice scar. He also inquired of almost everyone, "Did you know that you've got water under your knee cap? I do." But he almost didn't have. Donny believed himself to be immortal and invincible, it seemed he soon forgot his latest accident unless he was admiring his scars. However it was some time before he returned to his "tree home", and he left knives alone. The folks made that very clear. Again!

5

Trainers

Each spring Dad would take on the job of breaking two to four head of horses for other farmers. He would use our team of Molly and Queen to break the young horses to work in the fields. Dad would hitch the new horse next to Queen who was a big, unflappable strawberry roan horse that knew what her job was and did it well. She would brook no nonsense from any other horse young or old.

As her name stated she was the Queen. The young horses would try to pull away, ahead, back just about anything except go straight forward with no fuss. Queen would put up with their antics for a while then she would start by laying her ears back and threatening to bite. If the young horse did not heed her warnings then the next threat would become a promise and she would bite, usually on the neck. A few of these encounters and the young horse began to work like it was supposed to.

Once in a while Molly would act as though she had gone senile and Queen would put her in her place. Dad always said Queen was worth any two horses on the farm. Of course this was before he got his beloved Percherons. Before Donny and I got our own riding horses our parents would let us ride Queen over to Mom's parent's home. It was a four or five mile ride, and we thought we were big stuff to get to do this wonderful thing. Except we had to cross Dead Man's bridge and I always made certain it was not late afternoon when we returned home. I was afraid of the shadowed stone bridge under the tall old trees. Many years ago an old woman had actually found a dead man while she was picking blackberries. That didn't mean much to me, I was still afraid to go over the bridge on horseback.

We could not get off our horse between homes because we rode bare back and could not get back on. Once you got off on the way home you had to walk the rest of the way. Dad would not let us use the saddle. He had seen a man dragged to death when he was working in Oklahoma, and it left a lasting impression on him. It was two or three years before we were allowed to use the saddle.

Of these new horses Dad broke there was one or two that farmers also wanted trained to ride and that was what Mom loved to do. I would sit in the hay loft door and watch her work the riding horse. Or take the two little boys and stay in the wagon that was parked on the other side of the fence from where she was working. She could also see the little guys. We would take toys for the little boys and they would play on the floor of the wagon. I never got tired of watching Mom work with the horses. Jerry was so good about staying where ever we put him that it was never any chore to care for him, and Danny was very entertaining.

I never really learned how it was that Mom got the horses to accept the saddle and bridle, learn to carry grain filled sacks, jump over small obstacles and to go forward, backward and sideways on command. The one thing I did learn was that she never showed anger in the form of striking a horse. She would use blankets, grain sacks, buckets anything that made a noise to train the horse.

By the time she pronounced the horse trained and the owner came to ride it was afraid of very little. She would tie the saddled horse to a tree on the outside of the hog lot for a long time, so it could get used to the noise and smell of the hogs. Then she would ride the horses around and through the hog lot. She said that if the horse was spooky, hogs were a sure cure. I never saw a horse get serious about bucking her off she just never let them get that far ahead of her.

One young horse brought to us, (meaning our farm, but also Donny and I dreamed of keeping each one) was a colt with no name. I could not imagine having a horse and not giving it a noble name. Dad named the horse Billy after the man he belonged to. Billy! Donny and I wanted to give him a more exciting name than Billy. Dad reminded us that this little Morgan horse was not ours and we could not keep him and therefore we could not name him.

Billy lived up to his Morgan blood reputation. He could be worked right or left, with any other horse on the place and showed more common sense than some of the older horses Dad had retrained. Dad said some of the horses brought to him should have been shot and just be done with them as they were dangerous. They would bite, kick and rear up, just about anything to be rid of a human. Most of them Mom said had been mistreated.

Finally the day came when Dad felt he had taught Billy everything he could and made that report to Billy's owner. The owner was supposed to come and get him within the next few days. Much to Dad's disapproval Donny and I cried at the thought of losing "our" horse.

All too soon the day arrived when a truck pulled into the driveway. Dad sent us both scooting into the house. We had started crying as soon as we saw the truck. From the living room window we watched Dad snap a lead rope to Billy's halter and lead him into the yard. While the owner watched Dad picked up each of Billy's feet and held them a few minutes, hoof care was something the horse would not do when Dad got him. Dad tapped him on the side and the horse side stepped until Dad told him to whoa. The horse would back, come forward and stood perfectly still on command and to be harnessed.

Dad hitched Billy and Queen together and with the owner driving they went north down the road. Dad hitched Billy on the left side so he faced closest to the oncoming traffic. This was the hardest position for a young horse to accept and some took longer than others to accept working close to traffic. When they came back the owner did not appear to be very happy. Billy was definitely not the same horse the man had brought to Dad. So what was the problem?

As we watched the little horse work, Donny through tears that stained his face, kept saying over and over, "I wish he would bite that guy". Dad and the man stood and talked for a while then Dad did a very strange thing, he tied Billy to the fence post with Queen and came into the house where Mom was making dinner. They stood and talked for a short time then Mom went into their bedroom and we could hear her pulling the tin box from under the bed. Dad went back out to the truck where the man had gotten in and closed the door. We watched as Dad handed the man some money, talked for a while then he turned untied the horses and led them back through the lot to the barn. The man in the truck backed out of the drive and left.

Dumbfounded Donny and I ran to Mom both trying at once to question her. Her eyes were moist as she told us that Billy was ours. OURS, he belonged to us! We trampled one another getting outside to hug OUR horse. By the time we got to the barn Dad had un-harnessed the horses and turned them loose. We were so happy to see Billy heading out to pasture instead of leaving in that truck.

Years later I learned that the man didn't think much of the little horse. He believed that Billy should have grown to be much larger. He really did not know anything about the Morgan breed or he would have realized he had a jewel in a black coat. I also learned that the horse cost Dad his training fees and $75.00. What a bargain! He was our horse now but Dad would not let us rename him saying it was bad luck.

Now that we owned him Donny and I began to take more liberties with OUR horse. We would sit on his back while he ate in his stall at night, never in the morning for fear Dad would come into the barn. Dad broke the horses to work but Mom trained them to ride. She had started to train him to ride but she had not said he was ready for us to ride.

Getting braver we would catch him when he was out to pasture and out of sight of the house in the afternoon. One of us would ride while the other led him. After working all morning he was not hard for us to ride. Mom was also working him under saddle, but Billy never seemed to mind us riding him bareback.

Donny and I got brave enough to ride alone with just his halter. Next came riding double but we fought over who would "drive". Our secret came to an end one afternoon as we rode up along the Plum thicket that grew between the house and pasture. We were so careful not to leave the safety of the trees for fear Mom would see us. As we neared the trees there on the wagon tongue sat Mom and two grinning little guys. I can remember how my heart stopped, not for fear of punishment but afraid I'd never get to ride again.

Billy, Donny and I were motionless as Mom stood up and walked toward us. She took the halter lead in her hands and tied the loose end to the opposite side of the halter. The way we had it we could only turn him one direction. She was smiling as she told us, "just don't forget that when you use the bridle never jerk the reins, it won't take much to stop him." We were speechless and finally I found my voice and said something like "you mean we can ride him?" As if we weren't sitting up there already! He was to become one of the best horses I ever rode.

◦✐◦

Every late afternoon possible found us riding Billy. Donny and I thought to make up for him not getting to go out to pasture with the other horses, we should feed him twice the amount of corn and oats as Dad had told us to feed.

Mom and Dad unhitched their teams at noon and the horses were turned out unless Mom wanted a team for something. But usually after Dad went to work Mom would spend the afternoon canning, house chores and later in the day work in the gardens. The horses were usually left to pasture in the afternoon.

Dad noticed that Billy was gaining more weight than the other horses. He asked us about how we were feeding him his nightly meal. When we explained why Billy got double rations he was quick to explain to us that we were not to change the feed on any of the stock unless he told us to. Billy could not eat oats alone as he would choke. Donny and I made sure that we shelled ear corn and mixed the grain for Billy. Also Dad had put golf ball sized rocks in his feed box so he had to pick the grain out and eat slowly. And since I was the "official" egg gatherer I gave him a raw egg each night. It made his coat shine. Dad noticed that also. Billy's coat had been in poor shape when he came to Dad. Dad fed him raw eggs for protein and it made his coat sleek and shiny. He developed a taste for eggs.

⟡

One day Dad decided to ride Billy a mile up to the main road to get the mail. All the people who lived on our road had a mail box in a row of boxes across from the school house. Billy had not been ridden to the mail box and Dad thought it was time. Dad told Mom he would deliver the mail to an elderly couple Mr. and Mrs. Wolfe who lived on our road. Donny and I weren't very happy because he wouldn't let us ride Queen and go with him.

We sat on the well platform and watched them leave our drive. I thought Billy looked very graceful as he pranced along and Dad sat a horse very well. With his all-knowing face screwed up Donny proclaimed, "Billy don't like that saddle." When we rode him we never used the saddle but Mom used the saddle, so how did Donny know Billy didn't like it?

Sometime later the pair returned, both of them rather subdued. We later learned they had an altercation on the way home. It seems they had a misunderstanding about how fast to go, Billy bucked Dad off, went a short distance and began to eat grass. He wasn't in such a hurry after all. My Dad was not afraid of any horse I ever knew and Billy was no exception, so they had come to an understanding. A few more rides and then Dad started to let us ride Billy and Queen to the mail box. We were fast outgrowing Queen. We also noticed he referred to Billy as our horse, meaning Donny and myself.

The rest of that summer and for a few years to come was about as good as kids can have. We had a lot of chores to do but lots of time for our horses. The more we rode the braver we got. When Mom was a girl she had her own horse named Cricket. We loved for her to tell us stories about when she was a girl. She taught us to love horses as much as she did. Perhaps Donny got his ideas from Mom's stories. However, nothing she ever told us vaguely resembled the things Donny did. Mom told us a story that she had read of people in a circus who rode horses standing up on the horse's backs. Also they rode two horses at a time and it was called Roman riding. Donny thought this really sounded good, and convinced me that it could be easily done. Again we practiced down in the pasture.

Queen was an ideal candidate for our experiment because her back was broad and Billy didn't take to the idea very well. Not only was he not fond of a kid with pinching toes walking on his back, his coat was so sleek we couldn't stay on. The raw eggs might have had something to do with it.

Our game came to an end one day when Mom came to the barn to start chores, looked down the hill and there we were. She yelled, Donny lost his balance and we had our lives or at least our hides threatened if she ever caught us riding like that again. Once discovered the fun went out of our adventure and I don't believe we ever tried riding standing up again. Besides we were told that Dad was going to buy a pair of new horses so we started to dream of training them.

Once Mom sent Donny and me to our grandparents, Mom and Dad Richards, with a letter she had gotten from Uncle Ray who was in the Army overseas. After she and Dad had read the letter she passed it on for others in the family to read. Dad had taken the letter to work with him the night before so Mom's brothers and brothers-in-law that worked with Dad could read it. Aunt Vesta had a habit of keeping the letters and not passing them on so Mom wanted her brothers to read it first. She wanted us to wait until Mom and Dad Richards read the letter and then bring it home so she could give it to Uncle Charlie on Saturday night. He didn't work at the coal mine.

While Dad Richards sat in the living room reading the letter Donny and I sat quietly at the kitchen table. Our grandparents believed kids should be seen and not heard. Maybe we were hoping for a bread and jelly sandwich I don't know. Mom Richards sat a heavy crock on the table and dumped a chunk of square stuff that was white like lard. She stirred and mixed for a long time then she added a package of dark yellow stuff. She stirred and mixed some more until all the stuff in the crock was yellow.

I asked her what it was and she said it was Oleo, butter. It didn't look like any butter I ever saw made. My Mom used a gallon jar, poured heavy cream in and shook it in her lap in a rolling motion until small yellow balls appeared. She continued to "churn" the cream until the little balls clung together to form a large ball floating in buttermilk. She took the butter ball out of the jar and put it in cold water to wash the buttermilk from it, then mixed salt into it and dried it on a clean towel and pressed it into a special bowl with a lid. Then she sent me to the cellar to store it. She salted the butter milk and poured it into a jar that was also stored in the cellar. This she called sweet buttermilk. My Dad liked the buttermilk and drank glass after glass.

Mom used this method to churn our butter until Dad went to an auction somewhere and bought a gallon jar with a crank mounted on top of the lid and wooden paddles inside the jar. When you turned the crank the paddles turned. I was always fascinated to see the small yellow balls form then collect into a large ball. I always sat on the floor to churn then it wouldn't break if it tipped over.

Two of Moms brothers liked what she called rancid butter. She churned sour cream into butter for them. I don't know why their wives couldn't have churned the sour cream, but it seemed my Mom was always baking or cooking something for her family.

Before Donny and I returned home Mom Richards spread oleo on a couple of slices of store bought bread and put store bought jelly on it. Boy it couldn't hold a match to Mom's homemade bread, butter and her jelly. Of course Donny and I discussed this on the way home and we decided that Oleo tasted like lard and it left an oily coating in your mouth, the bread didn't have much taste and the jelly sure wasn't like Mom made.

Mom also made our cottage cheese. She would set two to four crocks of milk that would sour and turn to clabber (Dad also liked the clabber in a glass and drank it like milk.) When the milk was properly clabbered it would separate the milk from the water it contained. Mom drained off the water then put the clabber in a clean cheesecloth bag and hung it on the clothesline to completely drain all the liquid from it. When it quit dripping she put the clabber in a crock and mixed light cream salt and pepper with it. All of us liked this cottage cheese, and Uncle Charlie seemed to know when Mom made cottage cheese and took a jar of it home with him. My Dad ate his cottage cheese with sugar sprinkled over it.

In the winter time Moms brothers Buck, Charlie and George came to our place to hunt with Dad in the corn fields for rabbits. They dressed the game and washed it clean in a tub of water then they brought it in the house where Mom fried the rabbits, had biscuits or yeast rolls in the oven and made gravy for the men. Seldom did the wives come for these dinners.

The hay loft was a good place to watch Donny do his "training". He called himself a trainer as he broke calves and pigs to ride. He would drive his prey into the barn lot, close the side gates so that there was very little room for the animals to run and from there on it was Katy-bar-the-door. The pigs were the most fun to watch him ride if you could call it riding. He would manage to get the pig in the corner, scramble on and after a shrill squeal and a jump Donny would be face down in the dirt. He would get up determined to try again. This would go on for some time until either Donny or the pig had all the fun they could stand. Once the pig was tired it would just stand still grunt and squeal, at that point Donny would declare the pig trained and let it back into the hog lot. He never seemed to enjoy the pigs that were docile.

The calves on the other hand were easier to catch but hard to wear down. Bluff and blunder Donny would put a rope halter on the calf. Dad put halters on the calves at an early age so this was no real feat. Donny would corner the calf in one of the milk stalls and put a rope in the calf's mouth, then scramble up on its back. The duo would burst out of the barn door just below and to the right of the hay loft door. I had a very good view of the proceedings as I lay on a bale of hay. But you really had to pay attention or the excitement would be over before it had begun.

The calf would make a couple of jumps and buck and Donny would fly into the air and again land in the dirt. There were some calves that simply refused to enter the barn lot alone, and therefore were deprived of Donny's training ability. I often wondered how they fared in life being "untrained."

On the other hand there were those calves that fell for the old food-in-the-bucket trick and would follow him into his trap. One of these was a red and white bull calf that Donny really did train to ride. He was the envy of the neighborhood kids. These kids would come to see Donny ride the red and white calf. Mom and Dad knew Donny was riding this calf in the pasture but they never allowed the neighbor kids to ride. I think they knew those kids wouldn't bounce like Donny did.

During that spring and early summer Donny lived to ride his calf. Of course it had a name and a quite proper one at that, Bully. As time passed Donny rode Bully less and less until one evening Bully chased Donny over the barn lot gate. Donny hit the ground, butt first as Bully hit the gate head first. Mom saw this episode from the barn. A few days later a large truck came and took Bully and his like relatives for a ride, they never came back. Donny never mentioned missing riding this calf.

On our small farm horses were a big part of our livelihood. We always dreamed of riding each one that came to us. As we grew old enough to have our own horses we were in seventh heaven. The horse that I claimed was the black Morgan named Billy, a most intelligent little gentleman. Uncle Frank knew of some people who had a horse for sale, maybe he was trying to be redeemed from the goat fiasco.

Lady was the horse that Donny fell in love with. She had been broken to work double and to ride but she had some habits Mom did not approve of. She was a long legged blaze faced sorrel that was reputed to have been of race horse heritage and that suited Donny just fine. The fact that she could run like the wind fitted his lifestyle very well. Donny and I had numerous races in and out of the pasture. I don't think I ever won even one race. Donny would give me a head start, and as he and Lady passed me, Billy would invariably bite at her as she ran past, much to the glee of Donny.

Lady had a bad habit, when she was ready to quit playing she would head for the barn and try to rub the rider against the side of the barn. This did not bother Donny, as they headed for the barn he would get on his hands and knees on her bare back until she had gotten past the barn. Then he was careful not to go near the barn again. Mom did not approve of this and started work to break the habit which she accomplished quickly. Who knew riding the horse around and around the barn at a hard run until the horse got so tired she wanted to lie down and when she tried to get near the barn to rub Mom off Mom would yell at her. When Mom was finished with her Lady was as nice to ride as Billy was.

Dad rode Billy when he had time, Donny rode Lady and I rode Queen. We would go with him to check fields, fences and cow pastures. The river check was the best the field was about a mile round trip from the house and then we would ride around the field. We passed through a green tunnel most of the way to the field as the trees formed a canopy overhead. Two other neighbors that lived over east used this road to get to their field. It was an inconvenience for them and Dad had rented some of their river bottom land which was great for us.

The big orchard located across the road from our house was abandoned. The owner came once or twice during the time we lived there. He told the folks in the neighborhood to help themselves to the twenty or so acres of apples. One enterprising neighbor put up a cider press and made gallons and gallons of cider, year after year. Mom and Dad bought cider from him but it was not anything I cared for.

At the east end of the orchard was a pasture of fifteen or so acres that Dad rented. This was fenced in two parts and there were lanes on each side of the orchard back to the pasture land. Once during the time the cattle were in the back part of the pasture Dad discovered a very large bumble bee nest located in the center of the south lane.

He told us to go by way of the north lane to check the cows until he could get rid of the bees nest. Checking on the young heifers in the evening was one of the high lights of my day. We had to count the cows to make certain that none had gotten out and to pump water. Dad or Mom would check on them in the mornings. There was nothing I loved more than to ride the horses back to the pasture and then take the long way home. Regardless of how foolish the idea was Donny and I were never far apart.

On this particular day Donny wanted to check the haunted house. Where the idea of the house being haunted came from I don't know, since Mom and Dad laughed when we talked about it. At any rate the haunted house was located at the east end of the south lane and then back some distance off into a small grove of trees. We were told not to go to the old house because there was a couple of old wells and a cistern there. Dad did not want us fooling around the old house.

Donny insisted we could sneak past the bumble bees on the way down to the pasture, "they will be asleep when we come back." Somehow it made sense to me, except I stayed about two rows of apple trees out in the orchard till I was certain we had gone past them. I did not have to worry about knowing when we got past the bees, Donny's horse stirred up the nest. She took off in a hard run.

I made a wide detour around the bees. Donny had supposedly gone to the pasture and checked on the cattle (or so he said). He was traveling real fast but I think the horse just ran off with him. When I got back from the pasture it was my turn to pump water for the cows; he was at the haunted house when I found him. I was afraid to go near the house and called to him from the lane. I finally got brave enough to go closer to the haunted house. He had discovered one of the wells, and had taken some of the boards off the top to look in. I kept yelling at him to come on that we had to get home before dark. If an owl or large bird had flown from the upstairs of that old house I would have died on the spot!

In his hurry to get me to shut up he stumbled as he was putting the boards back over the well. Only the Lord above will ever know what kept him from falling into the well, except as usual God had sent an angel with a hand on Donny's shoulder. I got to him as he was getting to his hands and knees, his face was ghostly white. I know at one point all I could see was his lower body sticking out of the well. We were both shaking as we put the boards over the well top and rolled the big rocks into place.

It was a very subdued Donny that rode home that evening. He walked the horse out of the orchard past the bee nest. Mom thought he had come down with some illness when he took his bath and went to bed early and without supper. We did not go to the pasture by way of the south lane for several days and Donny didn't mention visiting the haunted house after that incident.

◈

During our trips back to the apple orchard pasture, it was not unusual for us to race. We had been told not to race the horses especially if the weather was hot. This particular time I guess it wasn't hot, because we were racing. As usual Donny had passed me as if I was standing still, but I had the last laugh.

As we reached the end of the orchard Lady shied as she was prone to do with some regularity. When she did her side step at a fast run all sorts of things could happen. This time it took the form of going under an apple tree. It was rather like a ballet, the horse gracefully did her buck and wing and left Donny hanging out in mid-air under the apple tree. Lady stopped and began eating grass.

I stopped my horse in his tracks. I was laughing so hard I was in no condition to fight off a mad brother. I slowly walked my horse to where Donny was getting back on. I never said a word, for all intent and purpose it was as if he had deliberately gotten off the horse to pick an apple.

✿

As Danny grew up his hero was Donny. So of course he decided to try his hand at "training" Billy. Danny would ride the little Morgan all around the barn lot. No matter how hard he drummed on the sides of the horse with his little pointy heels the horse never got out of a slow walk. After a short time of slow riding Danny became bored and turned to Donny for inspiration. Donny decided to show Danny a trick.

He put an apple in the hip pocket of Danny's overalls and showed Billy where the apple was. Billy was always looking for apples, so this was a snap. He would bite the apple in half and work the bite out of Danny's pocket. After a couple of apples Danny's pants would be wet and sticky, but he never seemed to tire of having Billy take apples out of his pocket. Now Danny was a horse trainer too.

Danny went on to learn to milk a cow. Milking as all farm chores was a family affair. We all went to the barn unless it was very cold, then one of us had to stay at the house with the two little ones. In fair weather we all went to do chores.

Like all little children who are too small to do chores, Danny couldn't wait to grow up enough to be a big kid and help with the chores. Don't ask me what he found appealing about having hogs knock you down as you tried to feed them or having a Tennessee Jersey cow AKA Miniature Jersey try to kick your head off. Dad would buy six or eight young heifers from cattle dealers and have them shipped in. After they had their calves and he and Mom milked them a few times he would declare them "broke" and Donny and I milked them.

Tennessee Jerseys are very small golden brown cows, with big brown deceiving eyes and very small teats. They were high grade cream producers. However her main goal in life, or at least the majority we came in contact with, was to try to kick the milk bucket into the rafters of the barn. Some of them were very good at it too. Their redemptive quality was the high butterfat content of the cream that was sold for butter.

While we milked Danny and Jerry played in their corn crib play pen with the door that opened into the milking area. The folks used the crib for overflow corn, which was leftover from the big crib. The corn was used from the small crib first, then swept clean and a few toys were put in there for the little guys, this made a perfect play pen. When the top door was open, the bottom door was chest high on Jerry. They had a ring side seat for all the activity in the milking barn. We could get about five cows in at one time. I can remember more than once after a cow had kicked the milk bucket out of my hand, looking up to see two giggling grinning faces from those two. But they were fast outgrowing their playpen.

Danny really wanted to learn to milk a cow. He finally talked Donny or vice versa, into teaching him to milk a big red cow that we had. Donny and I fought over who would milk her, because she was so gentle and so easy to milk. Danny would scramble out of the play pen so he could try his hand at milking. With several attempts Donny taught Danny to milk. Big mistake! The cow was so gentle and she would come to the fence where the little boys pulled grass for her. Of course it was the same grass as on her side of the fence but she ate it with pleasure.

One evening Mom and the four of us kids started for the barn. For some reason Mom stopped off at the baby chicken brooder house for a few minutes. She raised chicks from early spring till really cold weather the last ones were preserved by canning the meat for winter. Any stall from chores meant more playing time for Donny and me. When we finally got to the barn several cows were at the door ready to be let in. But we couldn't find Danny! Mom thought he was with me and I thought he was with her. Old Red was lying down contentedly chewing her cud, with her back to us. We heard familiar giggles as we walked up to her. There sat Danny on the ground, milking. He had milked a large puddle of milk and a couple of fat little kittens were having supper! Kid, cow and kittens were all happy.

After a lecture and not a very strong one (it was so hard for Mom to be serious when she was laughing) about wasting the milk she promised Danny that if he wouldn't waste the milk she would let him milk with us sometimes. After that we brought Old Red in first and let Danny milk till his little hands got tired. He would go back to the "play pen" a very happy little boy, to tell Jerry who was impressed, about how to milk a cow. It wasn't too long until we let Danny claim Old Red and Dad made a special stall so the other cows couldn't crowd her and we let Danny milk to his heart's content. He was one happy kid!

6

The New Team Arrives
and a Friend Leaves

Dad heard of a pair of matched grey horses that were for sale. Since he had rented land on each side of us he needed more horses to farm with. At this time we had Queen, Molly, Billy, Lady and whatever horses he was breaking. There was also a pair of mules that a neighbor wanted used to keep them working. The mules were kept in their barn adjoining our property. The man who owned the farm moved to Springfield when he got sick so the homestead was vacant for a while. The man did not want to sell his prize mules. My parents believed he wanted to someday be able to farm again when he got over his illness. After he passed away his daughter Eadie, her husband J.D. and Eadie's daughter Joanna moved into the house but it was empty for a couple of years.

Part of the deal for the grey team was for Dad to break a young horse named Barney. The truck arrived with two of the most beautifully matched iron grey horses, they were Percherons! They danced and pranced but didn't really give Dad any trouble. In my opinion getting new horses was like an enormous Christmas. Dad was so proud of this new team. He even took time to hitch them up before going to work missing his dinner. Dad was so pleased and so were Donny and I. The horses were so beautiful and it was hard for Donny and me not to think about "taming" them. However Dad gave us to understand that under no circumstance were we ever to fool around with the Percherons. He had no idea what we might teach them!

Mom really liked working the mules and got along better with them than Dad because he did not like mules. When Donny and I had work we could do our team was Queen and Billy. Dad made us responsible for our team and although we did the easy work it had to be done right or else. Dad and Mom had plans to enlarge our farm and we children were part of the plan.

Barney wanted no part of training, work or people. Someone had mistreated him so badly that to put a halter or bridle on him was a job. It seemed the more Dad worked with him the more stubborn he became. Sometimes he wouldn't come up from the pasture or go in the barn and never to his own stall. Sometimes it seemed he did not want to do anything asked of him. He was so obstinate. He did seem to be interested in us "little people".

Well, Donny and I couldn't have a horse like that around and not try to make friends with it. Donny referred this making up to the horse as "training him". Dad warned us severely not to tamper with the grey Percherons no one said anything about Barney. I think Dad supposed his kids had more sense after seeing the horse rear up and strike out. Wrong! Slowly however Barney came around. Donny and I would go to his pasture and get as close as he dared let us then we would sit down and act as though there wasn't a horse within a mile of us. We took apples to eat and threw the partly eaten apple to him. The horse was ever watchful. He would eat and watch us constantly never taking his eyes off us. He wasn't even a pretty horse by the standard of our own horses. He was bay with a few white markings, and he was so much stockier than our horses.

After a period of time of us feeding him apples in the afternoon he began to come closer to us. Dad turned all the horses together except Barney; he didn't even like other horses. Of course our own horses came as soon as they saw us we always had apples for them too. Barney somehow got three things in mind, one the other horses were not afraid of us, two that we always had apples and three he was bigger than these two little critters who tagged after him. Then came the day that as we went through the gate to his pasture he came to meet us. After what seemed a long time of doing this he finally let us put the halter on him. We were proud of ourselves and our "training" was going well. Every day now Dad was working him with Queen and from the start she made it clear how this partnership was going to work out. After a few lunges and several bites to his neck he settled down to business and worked. Donny Danny and I sat in the doorway in the hall of the barn and watched the goings on. This kept us out of the way and also we could get Mom if Dad needed her.

Of all the horses we watched Dad, break Barney was the most interesting. He would earn his pay for breaking this sturdy bay horse. After several days of working the horse on a sled that we used to pick up rocks in the field or haul water tanks on, he hitched Queen and Barney to a wagon. He felt so confident with Queen that he knew she wouldn't let him run. When she was working she was in no mood for nonsense.

The young horse had backed, turned and started on command well enough to please Dad, but when Dad backed them up to the wagon Barney stepped on the wagon tongue and broke it. This happened two or three times and it was so deliberate that finally Dad got mad and attempted to teach the horse a lesson. I always hated for any of the horses to get a whipping so I took Danny and went to the house. There was no problem if there was no tongue to the machinery but if he was hitched to anything with a tongue there was trouble.

During this time of "breaking him" Donny and I tried to do with Barney as we had with Billy. Barney wasn't as trusting as Billy but when he was in his stall we found that he appeared to like to have us brush and rub him. Finally Donny had enough of this TLC and decided it was time to get on with the business of "training". He climbed up on the side of the stall partition and slid over on the horses back. I really believe that if the horse had wanted to he could have pitched Donny into the hay loft as his stall was right on center. Donny did this once or twice a day staying longer and in general moving all over the horse. Barney seemed to like the squirmy crawling kid on his back and giving him apples didn't hurt either.

He now came to us when we called him. He still didn't get along with some of the other horses so he was kept in an adjoining lot alone. Maybe he was lonesome and kids were the last resort. Barney and Dad did not get along very well even as time passed. It was a daily battle between the two of them. The larger, stronger the wagon tongue, the harder Barney would stand on it trying to break it. It seemed the horse would actually bounce on it. Dad changed tactics. The team came along beside the implement and Queen stepped over the tongue, this worked well. But sooner or later Barney had to learn to do the same. It just seemed that backing up to the tongue was a bugaboo to the horse. In the mean-time Dad found that the horse worked very well on the swing side or hitched on either side just not to anything that had a tongue on it. Still he had to learn to work with implements with tongues. And so the battle continued.

Overtime Barney came around to being mauled by us kids, I believe he even enjoyed it. Mom worked him with the mules and would hitch him in the swing position. Then one day she hitched him to the wagon and left the team tied to a post for a long while. He finally learned to hitch to a tongue without incident. He would be going home soon.

Dad and Barney never became friends, just tolerated one another. With a high level of confidence we started catching him in the pasture and taking turns of one of us riding while the other one led him. We always fed him corn at the thicket because that's as far as we could ride without being seen. One thing we realized was that he never tried to buck us off. Again the day came when Mom caught us riding, we always believed Danny told on us because we wouldn't let him ride. He was about six or seven and of course we "older kids" knew best. She was not as tolerant about Barney as she had been with Billy. Our training came to an end; she said no more riding Barney. And we never did, but we continued to woo him with apples.

That summer was the beginning of a great sorrow for our family.

Dad got a contract to mow the right of way along Illinois State Route #29 between Edinburg and Sharpsburg. The work was hard for men and horses. Queen, Molly and Barney made up one team and the Percherons and Billy made up a second, with Lady as the alternate swing. Dad worked each team every other day from the time the grass was dry until about 1:00 pm. This mowing started about as soon as he got his crops in, but the State of Illinois set the date to start and finish.

Donny and I helped by picking up junk along the highway so the mower wouldn't break or dull the mower blades. With our too-big-for-us men's gloves we gathered the junk in a big pile and then the highway crew hauled it off. When Dad had to change or repair mower blades he cut off the rivets that held the blade onto the sickle bar. Donny would gather these rivet heads and place them on the railroad track that ran alongside route #29 and the train wheels ran over them. When the rivets were flattened the kids at school almost fought over them. Donny had a thriving trade going.

The necks of the horses got pretty sore by the end of the mowing season. The State of Illinois did not care what the reason was if you started mowing you fulfilled the season's contract or received no pay for the summers work. Dad said more than once he wished he had not gotten into that situation. Mom's brother Charlie used Dad Richards team and helped Dad with the mowing. This was some relief for our horses.

Part of our chores now was to doctor the necks of the horses at evening chores. Although their necks were sore none of them became as raw or bleeding as Barneys did. At this time Dad bought Barney from his owner. Donny informed me that he now had three horses, Molly Lady and Barney! And I only had two, Queen and Billy. I wondered who made him boss.

One morning as Dad was checking the horses he saw that Barney's neck was swollen and enlarged. He sent me to go get Mom. They lanced the sore spot and realized it was very serious. The spot was highly infected and eventually had maggots in the wound. The horse's necks had all healed except that Barneys had healed on the outside but not inside. We continued to pour iodine mixture over the wound twice a day, and Dad put some type of medicine he got from the veterinarian on his wound in the morning. The horse was not working but he got no better. Dad went for the veterinary. The vet did not come out that day and by the next day the horse was in serious condition. The vet told Dad that if the horse belonged to him he would shoot it. He took Dads money and left.

Dad and Mom could not kill the horse. They continued to use hot packs and pour the strong stinking medicine into the open wound. He was again in his old pen near the house. Mom doctored the horse several times a day now. For a time he appeared to get better. Then one evening Mom saw that he could not open his mouth, he had the dreaded lockjaw that goes with blood poisoning!

While we were pumping water for the stock he tried to come to the water tank. His legs were stiff and he wobbled from side to side. He could not lower his head, and held it high in the air. Mom led him back to the barn and to his stall. She then took the planks off the well platform and hauled up the water for the stock one bucket at a time so he could not hear the pump. When Dad got home from work he and Mom spent most of the night with little horse. At sunrise the next morning Dad went to get Mom's brother Uncle Buck to shoot the little horse as he was in such terrible misery.

Mom stayed with Barney near the barn in the shade where the horse collapsed. Crying, Mom was on her knees praying to God to please let the horse die before Dad and Uncle Buck got there. When she saw the cars drive up to the house she left the barn. Sometime later the men came to the house. Dad found his family crying, losing one of our horses was like losing a friend. Mom said she had not heard a shot, Dad put his arm around her and said Barney had died before they got there. We all missed the chunky little bay horse.

7

Field Work

After the chores were done and breakfast was over the family would head for the field. My favorite was the river bottom field Dad rented from a neighbor the third year we were there. It seemed to be a world all its own. Mom would make sandwiches from the leftover breakfast meat and biscuits. She would pack the wagon with blankets, water and toys for Danny and Jerry. Off she would go with the two little boys while Donny and I helped Dad take the extra horses to the field

One of the older neighbors had a pair of mules that he asked Dad to use in the field. The man could no longer work the mules and did not want them to forget the training. Dad and the mules did not get along, as Dad had an abiding dislike for mules. On the other hand Mom and the mules got along very well.

Donny and I would get to ride Billy and Lady and dream of being cowboys. Dad would usually take the other team and whatever implement he needed. If they were doing the same thing for a few days they usually left part of the equipment in the field. Once they were in the field they would each hitch three horses onto whatever piece of equipment they were using and go to work. Sometimes Donny would have me lead Lady once we got near the river and he would set fishing bank poles. He never had to worry very much about catching fish, where he was allowed to fish was a sand bar, no fish.

By the time Mom and Dad had their horses ready to work the sun would just be coming through the trees along the river, making long westward shadows. When the sun had reached mid-morning in the sky, they would have several hours of work in and a snack fed to everyone. Both little boys, if I was lucky, would have a nap under a blanket anchored over the top of the wagon for shade. I stayed near the wagon reading or practicing crocheting or embroidery that Mom was teaching me.

The folks would quit in time for Mom to go to the house to finish dinner. She would leave some type of meat and vegetables in the oven while we were gone. She and I would leave before Dad and Donny. Dad would quit in time to take care of the horses, eat dinner and get ready to go to work at the coal mine.

One spring after we had lived on Christian Forty for two or three years, Mom was using the mules to plow and she had an accident. There was a low water wash in the area of the field she was plowing. She had the mules and another young horse on swing. They had crossed the low ditch several times. At one point when they came to the ditch the young horse jumped causing the plow to run up on the mule's heels. That scared the mules and they ran off, turning the plow over pinning Mom underneath. She held onto the driving lines and the team began to circle into the plowed ground.

Dad saw what had happened and turned his team in their direction. The mules stopped within a short distance. Mom was banged and bruised pretty badly and for several days she stayed out of the field. When she got over her injury she went back to farming, with the mules. She was adamant that the mules were not at fault, and the young horse didn't know better. We had problems the same as any small farm but Mom and Dad always said the good would out weight the bad. One of Moms favorite sayings was, "if it weren't for the valley lows the mountain highs would not be as good."

Anything to do with farming and I was for it. I loved the smell of newly turned earth, spring rain, the dusty smell of summer, new mown hay and frosty autumn leaves. Dad took Donny and me and no bare feet we had to wear our shoes to shuck corn. We thought we were really grown up. He used the roan and bay mares Queen and Molly or Queen and Billy but not usually the team of grey Percherons unless he had to.

Cockleburs in the corn field were a real problem. Since the Percherons had a lot of hair called "feathers" on their legs it was hard to comb the burrs out. Dad would put nose baskets on the horses to keep them from eating corn and he would tie their tails up in a bundle and cover the tails with a piece of gunny sack so they did not get burrs in them. Donny and I took the row next to the wagon and Dad took the two rows farthest away from the wagon. The ears were head high to knee cap low. Donny loved it when he threw an ear of corn and it hit the bang board. Smug look took on a new meaning.

Dad seemed pleased that Donny and I shucked one row while he shucked two. I always got anxious when we came to the gate and I had to open it. Another time Dad had asked me to open the gate as we were leaving the field in the spring. I jumped off the wagon and ran to open the gate. As I stepped up to the gate bar suddenly something squeezed my foot and ankle hard, I had stepped on a big Black snake and it wrapped it's self around my foot and leg! I screamed bloody murder also called the Banshee scream. Dad came running and pulled the snake off me. I can still remember not being able to stop screaming and shaking as Dad carried me to the wagon. Dad walked through the gate holding my hand several times before I could go alone. It was ever so long before I would walk through the gate without being scared even in winter when common sense told me the snakes were hibernating.

I believe I had such a terrible fear of snakes because Mom was afraid of them. She had reached into her clothes pin bag one time while hanging up laundry outdoors and there was a snake in it. I also inherited her need to kill snakes. I was a grown woman before I finally overcame the fear and could actually touch one.

❧

When the wheels on the horse wagon became squeaky or wobbly because they had dried out in the hot summer sun, Dad would drive the wagon into the river where there was a gravel bottom. He would move the wagon just enough each day to turn the wheels so the whole wheel was in the water for a while. Soaking the wheels would make the wood swell and tighten the wooden spokes by expanding them and the metal band would tighten up. Dad would also load the wagon with gravel and spread it in the drive way. When we first moved to Christian Forty he hauled innumerable loads of rock and gravel and made a solid drive way. In later years a load ever two or three years plus the stove ashes kept it in good shape.

❧

Mom and we four kids spent our evenings in various ways. After the corn was shucked Dad picked out the best ears and we would shell the corn for seed corn. Mom would spread an old sheet on the floor and when we had the seed corn shelled we spent a few nights shelling corn for the chickens. Later Dad borrowed a corn sheller from Dad Richards or he would take the corn down there and shell it. We always listened to the radio while we worked. No one we knew had TV when I was a kid, we had never even heard of it. Everyone got their news and entertainment by radio or newspaper. Once in a while Donny worked in silence while we listened to the radio, but not often.

❧

One evening Mom produced a little green package that she opened and gave each one of us a wrapped stick of chewing gum. I loved the smell of Wrigley's double mint gum. Mom was careful to explain that we were to chew the gum but not to swallow it. Donny paid no attention to Mom's instructions. He chewed his gum and promptly swallowed it. Of course whatever Donny did Danny had to do also. Jerry's gum ended up in his hair, we never knew how he managed that. Suddenly chewing gum disappeared from our lives for quite some time.

One evening Mom and I and the two little boys came into the house after chores, we did not know where Donny had taken himself off to but it was pretty certain that he would come in when it got dark. Mom set about fixing supper and the two little guys and I got busy with whatever had their interest at the moment. Still no Donny. Finally Mom went into the living room for something and there sat Donny on the floor watching the telephone. It was something new for us and had only been installed for about a week. Mom called her parents a time or two and they called her when they needed something. This stopped the trips Donny and I made to their house with letters now that Mom and her parents could talk on the telephone. It was a wonderful invention but I missed riding the horse to deliver messages.

Mom said, "Donny what are you doing sitting on the floor?"

His answer was "I am watching for the telephone to ring." Mom shook her head and returned to the kitchen. At least he was in the house and quiet.

8

Family

The war called World War II included people from all walks of life and at least one member from each family. The war was a constant source of conversations when family gathered or neighbors visited. In our family Uncle Ray, Cousin Jimmy and Cousin Buddy were all in the service. Families awaited the latest news from the men. If the family did not receive a letter in a timely fashion there was much anxiety until one did arrive.

We had studied maps in school and I knew that the war was being fought in Europe. At times when we were at our grandparent's home and the news commentator Gabreal Heater came on the radio everything came to a halt, a silent halt! Everyone, adults and children alike must be quiet. There was always a war report and since Uncle Ray and the cousins were somewhere overseas all the adults were glued to the radio, praying there was word the war was over. Of course Mom's youngest sister Vesta and the family "baby" would have seen a news reel at the movies. She and her dates went to the movies three or four times a week. She had to tell everyone what they were hearing and even Dad Richards couldn't make her shut up. She was not one of my favorite aunts, she was abusive and overbearing to everyone.

When I was about ten years old Uncle Charlie came to our home one afternoon, he and Mom talked very quietly and Mom began crying.

Uncle Charlie helped us do chores although it was not chore time. We didn't milk all the cows only the ones that did not have calves. Mom said to turn the cows and calves together, we fed the horses, chickens and hogs.

She got all of us kids cleaned up, but she couldn't stop crying and I knew something terrible had happened, all I asked was if Dad was alright and she said he was but gave no further explanation. Uncle Charlie sat on the bench under the tree in the front yard, his head in his hands. Once all of us had gotten cleaned up Mom sat us down on the sofa in the living room and told us we were going to go to Mom and Dad Richards. She said Uncle Ray had been killed on February 25th, 1945, but the family had just received word of his death

Uncle Ray was a tank gunner and his tank had been bombed. Mom told us the family was gathering at our grandparent's house. I asked if Dad would be there and Mom said no, that since Dad worked with Uncle Ray's brothers and they were called home, Dad and Uncle Frank and Uncle Teed would have to work until more men could be called in. She said he might even have to work overtime. I just felt a tremendous need for all of my family to be together.   Mom explained to us that when we got to our grandparents home we were to be on our best behavior, that I was to look after Danny and Jerry and that Donny was to be quiet and behave himself. We all knew this was serious because we had not seen Mom crying for a long time, since baby Carold died.

When we got to our grandparents home Mom's other brothers and sisters and their families were there all except Vesta. The four of us kids and Uncle Buck's five younger kids were told to sit on the side porch off the kitchen. We could hear quiet sobs from the living room. The setting sun began throwing long shadows across the yard putting the porch in semi darkness.

A car none of us recognized drove up the driveway. It was Aunt Vesta and a man, her latest boyfriend, none of us knew. She ran flailing her arms and screaming into the house while the man wandered down to the pasture fence that bordered the south side of the yard. He stood watching Dad Richards cows for a while then returned to his car to sit.

He said nothing to us but remained in the car for some time. Finally he started the motor of the car and backed out of the drive way.

Inside the house we could hear hysterical screaming and crying. Aunt Vesta was in full hysterical mode. Mom brought us cookies and stayed with us for a while. The men, Moms Dad and her brothers and Uncle Lester had been sitting in the kitchen, they soon came outdoors. Dad Richards went to stand by the pasture gate at the far end of the yard. Mom's brothers did the milking and chores for Dad Richards. Mom took all of us kids and walked out to where he stood. Mom put her arms around him and he seemed more like a child than her father. Mom took all of us back to the house and started preparing supper for everyone. When she had the meal prepared she had all the children come into the kitchen and fill their plates then we went to the back porch where there were benches that we set our plates on and kneeled while we ate. The sun was going down casting a red glow on all of us children as we quietly ate our supper in a strange silence.

The adults filled the big kitchen to eat. Aunt Vesta suddenly re-membered the boyfriend and went out to have him come in to eat. When she realized his car was gone she demanded us kids tell her where he had gone, of course we had no idea. She began to scream and cry again. When Mom and some of the women got the dishes done she made pallets on the floor in the living room for the smallest children. The rest of us lay down near our little brothers and sisters. All of us kids were at a loss as our world had been turned upside down at least that is how I felt. Donny and Eddy Gene who were always looking for adventure sat quietly in a corner whispering.

About midnight Dad got to Mom and Dad Richards home with Uncle Frank and Uncle Teed to collect their respective families. Some of the families had already gone home. Dad was visibly shaken over Uncle Ray's death. The family was notified that his body could not be sent home until later. In fact it would be more than four years before my uncle could be laid to rest permanently. My family had four years left to live a good normal life.

As the weeks and months passed the family's lives began to return to normal but when there was any family gathering Uncle Ray's life was talked about, and laughter and tears and a lot of love came out. Mom still had two nephews, Jimmy and Buddy in the army. All the families listened close to the radio and there was much talk of the war progress. Germany in desperation was fighting a hand to hand combat. We heard of places with German, Russian, Poland, French names and still the war did not stop. On December 7, 1941, a place called Pearl Harbor had been bombed. The United States declared war on Japan and for almost four more years the war raged on. Then two new names became places everyone was talking about, Nagasaki and Hiroshima in Japan. The United States had bombed the towns, but no word as to the end to the war.

One day the four of us kids were playing in the front yard when the teenage neighbor kids named Tucker came yelling and running down the road, they lived where Uncle Buck and Aunt Clara had once lived. They were racing to the south neighbor who were their friends or relatives. At this time the elderly neighbor man had died and his daughter Eadie, granddaughter Joanne and her step dad J.D. Higgins had moved in that summer to his house. Joanne came up to play with us but she had severe diabetes and could not play long. As the Tucker kids ran past our home they shouted for us to tell Mom that the Japanese had surrendered. The war was over, it was August 1945, and school would start in a couple of weeks.

One evening after supper Mom told us she had something to tell us. Of course we were all ears, maybe we were going to town for something special or we were going to go visit some friends that their Dad worked in the mine with our Dad. We did that sometimes, the families sharing pot luck suppers.

Mom didn't keep us waiting. She told us that this coming summer we were going to get a new little brother or sister. Of course Donny became vocal stating he wanted a brother as if ordering a pound of cheese. I was hoping for a sister, I was outnumbered by boys already. Mom showed us some of the baby things she had been crocheting. I was so surprised, I had been sitting alongside of her while she worked but had not seen the articles she spread out on the table. Soon after she told us about the new baby she began sewing tiny shirts and blankets and other things for the baby. All our thoughts now centered on the little new comer.

Dad was strict saying Mom was not to lift or carry anything heavy. Donny and I were old enough to do the milking and carry the milk to the cellar. Mom continued to work in her garden but most of the outside work was done by Dad and Donny and me. Of course Danny and Jerry wanted to help so we found chores they could do. We were all so happy and our life was good.

One evening during a heavy rain storm Mom went to the cellar to operate the cream separator. As she hurried the two little boys ahead of her out of the storm she slipped and fell down the steps to the floor of the cellar. She was seriously hurt and could not get up. I remember the fear when Danny came to the barn lot gate and screamed for me. I ran as fast as I could to the cellar and found Mom white faced and crying on the floor. She had hit the table where the cream separator stood and hurt her head, arm and shoulder. She was in a lot of pain. Between Donny and me we helped her to her feet and got her into the house. She kept insisting she was alright but she was so white and I was really scared. She insisted that Donny and I finish the chores that the two little boys would take care of her. When I came in from chores she was still lying down but she had all sorts of toys and two little boys on her bed.

Our suppers usually consisted of dinner leftovers so supper was no problem and Mom allowed me to carry a plate to her, but she ate very little. I was very scared I had never seen my Mother like this.

The next day the doctor came and shooed all of us except Dad from the room. Mom was very sick. For more than a week she stayed in bed, Dad did the cooking before going to work. Danny and Jerry took care of Mom while Donny and I did evening chores and they were so proud of themselves. As time passed Mom recovered but she was so quiet, no laughing or songs and finally one evening she put away the baby things she had made and told us there would not be a new baby. There was no explanation. It took her a long time to get back to herself and our lives went on again.

※ ※ ※

Dad's sister Ruth and her kids came to visit one afternoon. They seemed to appear on baking day and would load their car with eggs, bread and garden vegetables. They never put out a garden or raised any kind of farm animals to better themselves. There were several children in their family, one was a girl named Sarah after Dad and Aunt Ruth's mother. I seldom had another girl to play with so I remained in the house with her. Donny and Harold, who was about fourteen or fifteen years old, went off on their own adventure.

At some point when no one was paying attention the two sneaked Billy and Lady out of the pasture and went for a ride. During their ride they went north towards the school and they started to race the horses. I am certain Harold did not know how to ride since he had to use the saddle and my aunt and uncle did not own horses. They raced to the intersection of the east-west road which had just been oiled. Harold not knowing how to ride or too dumb to think what he was going to do when he reached the intersection and turned the corner at a run. Billy's feet went out from under him and he fell.

Mom discovered the boys and the horses were gone about the time they got back to our drive. They were walking and leading the horses. Billy was limping badly and had several cuts. Lady didn't appear any the worse for wear. Harold didn't look too good with road oil all over him. He showed no signs of injury in fact they were talking and laughing until they were discovered then Harold began to limp and whine. Aunt Ruth rushed to baby her eldest which she did often and could always find an excuse for his bad behavior.

Mom was mad, not simply angry but mad. When Aunt Ruth began

to blame the horse, Donny and God for her sons imagined injuries Mom blew up. Our horse was hurt by a very foolish act that was none of his doing and the horses were taken out of the pasture without permission. Aunt Ruth blamed Donny for that. Aunt Ruth continued to fuss and blame and finally gathered her brood saying she needed to get Harold to a doctor. A Doctor! All of us had been hurt worse without even the benefit of iodine and band aid. Harold was moaning and rolling around on the ground although he had walked the mile back to the house. The fool was careful to stay in the grass and not get in the gravel during his exhibition. As they left he was well enough for Aunt Ruth to let him drive the car. Whining would get whatever he wanted from her.

Donny was sent to sit on the porch, which he hated to do but he was in more trouble than he could talk his way out of this time. Mom took care of the horses and doctored Billy. Later Donny was told he was not to get on any horse until she said he could and he had more than usual chores to do. To his credit he was truly sorry that Billy was hurt. He later confided to me that Harold called him a sissy for not wanting to take the horses out of the pasture and somehow I understood how he felt.

Aunt Ruth continued to pamper Harold well into adulthood until he finally got into serious trouble. The incident was whispered about when Dad's family gathered and it appeared liquor and women were involved. Again it wasn't his fault according to Aunt Ruth.

Mom didn't get angry often but when it came to foolish people that caused harm to animals then she could boil over. Billy recovered without any ill effects to his legs and I kept close watch over my horse when we had company. Donny had learned his lesson since he wasn't allowed to ride until Billy was healed and all the road oil was combed from his coat. Not getting to ride was about the worse punishment he could get.

❧◦❧

Almost every Sunday from early spring Moms family came to our house for dinner especially when the chickens reached frying size. A couple of my aunts declared how they "just could not stand to kill those chickens" but it never bothered them when the chickens were cooked to a golden brown and stacked high on platters on the table. And they were "just too full to move" by the time the dishwashing was started.

One Sunday among the company was Moms brother Buck and his family. We were lucky they lived several miles from us in a small town, since Eddy Gene and Donny managed to do all sorts of dumb things and the girls were the guinea pigs. These cousins had a countrified mentality. They were not afraid to get dirty nor were they afraid of the animals. The two city cousins did not play outside. Norma Jean didn't want to get dirty and she didn't like the animals. Whatever she did Freddie was told to do also.

On this Sunday there was a wagon running gear in the barn lot. Dad had bought it to build a wagon bed on. The two boys pulled it around the lot then got the idea that it would be fun to ride it down a small hill in the pasture. They talked us girls and our little charges into sitting on the wagon frame. Florence and Delores held their little sisters Rita and Carol. I held Jerry, Danny wouldn't let anyone hold him he was getting to be more like Donny all the time.

The boys assured us the wagon would not go past the small dip in the pasture. We did this a couple of times and it was fun. And then they tied a rope on the tongue to hold it up. We all got on the running gears and the boys pushed it to get us started then jumped on when they got it rolling. No one thought of how to stop the silly thing. When it got to going fast the two boys jumped off! We went flying down the hill, bouncing and bumping all the way! The wagon did not stop at the dip it went all the way to the creek, stopping just short of the water.

The Lord was with us that day, had that rope broke and the tongue dropped to the ground there would have been kids on the moon to greet the astronauts. Mom always said the Lord took care of children and fools. That was certainly true, we girls were fools to listen to our brothers and the four little kids needed special care just by having us for babysitters. Of course one of the little kids had to tell excitedly about our ride. After the parents were satisfied we were all ok and all the kids were herded back into the yard there were threats of our punishment. Aunt Lena looked very smug and told Mom "I told you so." She could be smug her two kids were in the house.

⚜

Dad and Uncle Buck, Uncle George, Uncle Jim, Uncle Teed and Uncle Frank worked nights in the coal mine together. Eddy Gene thought that since his Dad was gone he had to "protect" his mother and siblings. He and Donny were always comparing notes on "what if". It was always dramatic and of course woe to the demons they were fighting. Donny was usually in cowboy or save the world mode; that is when he wasn't doing something that could almost get him killed.

Eddy Gene decided to help himself in his role of protector by setting a trap to catch any intruders. He stretched a rope across the walk and tied tin cans onto the rope. The theory being an intruder would run into the rope, rattle the cans which would wake Eddy Gene. Now up to this point I understood the reasoning which is scary. If Eddy Gene was awakened by his alarm what was he going to do about it? We would never know.

Uncle Buck went home to a dark house as Aunt Clara didn't usually wait up for him. No one had outside lights in small towns. Tired from a long night's work he headed for his back door, walking into Eddy Gene's trap. As the story goes, his hat, lunch bucket and jacket went one direction and my uncle went another. The racket produced caused the dogs in their neighborhood to set up a howl and I imagine Uncle Buck had a few choice words that turned the air blue. According to Eddy Gene he was in deep trouble. I am glad I wasn't there as I am not fond of thunder and lighting.

9

Feathers

On any farm the animals have to be a paying proposition or they do not stay around very long. Besides the garden, orchard, raising chickens and helping Dad farm, Mom also raised geese and ducks. She and Dad built a sturdy woven wire fence around about an acre and a half that included a small pond. Their next project was to clean out the pond and plant grass seed in the pen. From my point of view geese and ducks were a big improvement over hogs any day. Dad had rented another twenty acres from our neighbor south and it was set up for hogs, and that was how Mom got her large geese/duck pen. Dad still kept the sows with young babies close to the barn until he felt they were old enough to move. The hogs were moved south to a larger pen, more mud and an improved way to feed swill. It was farther for Dad to haul the milk to make the swill but he wanted to get it farther from the yard.

Mom also sold goose and duck eggs to the neighbors, they were in great demand. During winter holidays she butchered, cleaned and sold geese and ducks. It was nothing to see her cleaning fowl in falling snow. In the spring she would set a broody hen and have baby geese or ducks and not have to go through the hassle of being pecked by a mad gander or drake. It was easier to set chickens to hatch the eggs, since the ducks and geese insisted their nests be hidden around the pond. It became a game to try to find the hiding places of the geese and ducks.

They were free to roam their pasture and feed lot so anywhere became a nest site, and they came back to their nest to lay eggs. When the babies were ready to go to the pen they had their flight feathers clipped, and turned into their pen with parents they had never seen.

Dad bought a small building at the neighbor's sale and moved it into a smaller pen. By cutting a door in both ends of the building and one door set next to a space cut in the fence we could go into the pen. The ducks and geese were fed in this pen and kept overnight and were let out in the morning. With the addition Mom could raise several more pairs of geese and ducks. Still there were always those who managed to nest outside. Mom broke these nests up so the ducks and geese would roost inside otherwise foxes found them fair game. The snow and rain runoff kept the pond full. It didn't take us kids long to realize the goose and duck pen was no place to wander. There was always one gander or drake on the warpath who did not like kids.

At the end of the front yard near the road grew a seven sisters rose bush. At one time the bush was in the yard, but as years passed the owners who lived there before us had let it flow over the fence and onto the ground inside the orchard. The ducks and geese found this to be an ideal place to hide their eggs from marauding kids. Not so! Mom saw where they went and Donny and I took turns going in after the eggs.

The plan and Donny always had a plan, saying he knew all about geese, well he knew about some geese. The opening into the rose bush was on the orchard side so the plan was that I had to drive the geese and ducks down to their pond while Donny crawled inside the rose bush and gathered the eggs. I honestly did not see the old gander turn back. I thought I was doing very well with my flock gathered at the pond. I knew the plan had gone wrong when I heard the Banshee scream, and Mom started to yell, waving her apron over her head.

The gander sneaked back to the nest and got inside while Donny was still in there. Now if you have never had the experience of being bitten and flogged by an angry goose or duck, let me just say you should thank your lucky stars. Geese and ducks do not only beat you with their wings and rake with their feet but their flat beaks clamp onto skin and while they are pinching they also twist the skin. A little bit of this stuff goes a very long way. When Donny saw the gander coming into the rose bush he made a new opening out the other side, leaving the egg basket right where it was.

Donny looked like he had been in a cat fight! The gander strutted back to the pond, squawking all the way. Mom got the hoe and using it as a hook got the egg basket. I think I would have been forgiven IF I had not laughed at the way Donny looked. He had pieces of dried rose bush in his hair and his face and arms were scratched. I remember saying something about him looking like he had fought with a tom cat and laughed. Big mistake! The next thing I knew Donny flew at me like a mad gander, and I looked about as bad as he did. Not so funny now!

⟶ ∞ ⟵

Once Mom sent Donny to help me gather the chicken eggs, I think it was more to keep him occupied than I needed help as this was one of my chores that I enjoyed doing. I very seldom had any problems with the hens, so what had I done to deserve the help of this two legged mischief maker?

As we entered the hen house Donny flipped himself inside the door and flattened himself against the wall just like he had seen in the movies. He rolled his eyes at me and put his finger to his lips for me to be quiet. I don't believe the hens had ever complained about the noise I made. As I watched, my brother tip toed and slid along the wall towards the nesting area.

The hen house had individual nesting boxes in a row fastened to the wall about three feet above the floor of the building. There was a narrow shelf in front of the nesting boxes and an empty space under the nests. As I watched Donny dropped to his hands and knees and began to crawl under the nests to the back nest at the far end of the building. As Donny made his silent, secretive way to where ever he was going I began to gather eggs from the nests at my end. There were two or three hens still on the nest. If the hens weren't broody they would leave the nest when you approached. One hen left her nest with a loud protest that drew a frown from Donny.

I was almost finished when Donny slinked out from under the nest boxes. He stood up and flattened himself against an empty box as best he could. The nest on his right had a hen on it. His theory was not to let the hen see him. Without looking around Donny slipped his hand under the hen, she wasn't happy to have a scrawny little hand invade her territory and reacted with a squawk and a peck at the offending arm. The famous Banshee scream filled the hen house sending the chickens for the door. When I got to Donny he was trying not to cry muttering to himself and rubbing a round blue spot on his arm where the broody hen had pecked him.

Mom got to us about the time we got outside. She assured Donny that no one she knew of had ever died from a hen pecking their arm. I did not recognize the story when Donny related it to Danny and Jerry but he was the hero that saved me from the broody hen. I never had to worry about Donny taking my job he was not fond of gathering eggs.

❧ ❦ ❧

Each spring Dad and Mom would clean the chicken house and white wash the building inside and out. The chickens were caught and dusted with a powder to keep them healthy. Donny and I were never allowed to help with the dusting but the white washing was just a part of our job.

While Mom and Dad worked inside, they were smart enough to place Donny and me on opposite ends of the oblong building. We all worked on the chicken house to be ready for the new batch of baby chicks. This time I was on the west end of the building and I could hear Donny singing, I didn't think he could carry a tune in a basket with the lid on it, but there he was at the other end singing at the top of his lungs. He was doing a Gene Autry song loud enough to wake the dead, or at the very least cause the milk cows to go dry. Through the din of my brother's questionable musical talent I heard another sound that was pure joy. I heard a kitten.

Putting my brush down I went to the back gate to listen. The sound was coming from the Plum thicket that ran north and south along the hog lot. Again I heard the kitten cry. I was really terrified the hogs would find it and since I was convinced that hogs ate kids I was sure the kitten did not stand a chance. I went through the back gate into the barn lot, crawled under the barbed wire fence into the pasture that ran adjacent to the hog lot.

I had no fear of the horses or cattle so I went along their side of the thicket which grew on both sides of the separating fence. I could hear the kitten but I couldn't find it. Walking up and down on the outside of their fence drew the attention of several sows. I was frantic to find the kitten before they did. To no avail I ran back and forth calling to the kitten and the sows followed along on their side of the fence. After several minutes I began to cry I just knew the kitten would die in the jaws of the sows. I ran back to the chicken house to get Mom or Dad to help me. Mom had gone into the house to check on Danny and Jerry who were napping. Through a crying babble I told Dad of the lost kitten and what was sure to be its fate. He went with me to find the lost baby and as we neared the thicket we could hear the kitten cry.

The sows had lost interest and returned to their mud wallow. Dad motioned me to silence as we walked along the Plum thicket. Again we heard the cry of the lost kitten. Taking hold of my arm Dad pulled me over in front of him and stooped low to point into the trees. I could not see the kitten. I did see a little grey bird hiding in the dense leaves. Dad told me to watch the bird. Standing motionless we watched as the grey bird blended into the trees and hopped from branch to branch. Suddenly we heard the sound of the kitten again.

Dad told me that there was no lost kitten, that what I heard had been a Catbird and that I was not the first person to be fooled into thinking the sound was that of a lost kitten. We returned to our work and I was very happy - no lost kitten - and I had learned about another bird. Usually it was Mom who taught us to recognize the birds and their calls but I realized that Dad was pretty knowledgeable about birds also.

That same evening as we went to the barn to do the chores, again I heard the lost kitten cry of the Catbird. I did not really intend to fool Donny but when I simply said, "I think I hear a kitten," he handed me his milk bucket, climbed the gate into the hog pen, there was never a hog on the place he would admit to being afraid of. He ran along the Plum thicket, back and forth calling to the "kitten". There was not a sound until Donny came to the near end of the thicket. He became frantic, and refused to hear me as I called to him.

I took the milk buckets to the barn and told Mom about the Catbird. She told me to stay with the two little boys who were in their "playpen" in the corn crib. The top half of the door was open and the children stood looking out wondering what was going on that they were missing. They returned to playing and I started to put feed in the cow's boxes.

Mom smiled as she left the barn and went towards the Plum thicket. I went to the open end of the barn and watched as Mom and Donny slowly went along the west side of the trees to about the same place where Dad had shown me the Catbird. I saw Mom point into the thicket of trees.

Later that evening Donny proceeded to inform me that I was just a "dumb ole girl" that couldn't tell the difference between a kitten and a bird. "But I wasn't fooled" he boasted.

The rest of the summer and my life for that matter I would always remember that the Catbird was a great little imitator. You have to be very quiet and patient to get a glimpse of this secretive little bird, but the reward is well worth the effort.

The seasons of spring and autumn were my favorite times of the year. Summer was good and I never really liked winter although both of these seasons had their good times also. I loved the blaze of color in autumn with the warm days and cool nights. Spring was a total joy - new baby animals were everywhere. It seemed as though each new day brought new babies; calves, colts, kittens and chicks. I liked baby pigs but only until the cute wore off.

Mom would place an order with the local feed store for baby chickens. When they arrived we would go to town and bring them home in boxes with dime size holes cut in the sides they had been shipped in. Mom would work for days before the chicks arrived to get the brooder ready. It had to be snug and warm, as baby chicks are delicate little things.

A kerosene lantern was hung from a heavy wire hook attached to the ceiling of the brooder for both light and heat. It was fun to just watch the baby chicks run, eat and drink. For the first two or three weeks they would be confined in a small area then set free into a larger pen when they were a little older. Danny and Jerry loved to watch them but I had to stay with them, otherwise baby chicks were "set free" to run everywhere.

Mom excelled at raising chickens, ducks and geese. Her chicken flock was made up of several breeds. Buff Orpingtons were great gold birds that were good meat and egg producers also the Plymouth Rocks. Both of these chickens laid large brown eggs, and were a gentle breed. I never minded gathering their eggs even when the hens were trying to set. Mom used these hens to hatch the duck and geese eggs, as the hens made better mothers and less work than the ducks and geese who ran free.

The Rhode Island Reds were Moms favorite because she said they could out lay the other chickens even in winter. She sold dozens of eggs. She also had some Leghorns because she had some customers that did not want brown eggs, and then there were the Bantams, fondly called Banties. They were the feisty, colorful fighters. Someone gave a pair to us kids and as anyone knows who has ever had any truck with Banties, a hen and a rooster and you are bound to be overran by Banties. They are prolific under the most adverse conditions!

Mom was not fond of Bantams, they never stayed where they were put and were pretty flighty. They were little, but they were good mothers. The roosters were very territorial and they were almost as good a look-out as the Guineas were. Dad had traded someone a pair of ducks for the Guineas and they lived in the Plum thicket and were there to warn of foxes, or other varmints that had chicken on their minds for a meal.

Each year we would end up with lots of Bantam chicks. The neighbor kids all wanted Banty chicks so we just gave them away. Mom was careful to give away as many as she could. I believe she thought by giving them away the original pair would finally live out their life, and we would be rid of the little rascals.

Each of my brothers and I were allowed to pick out a pet chicken. Usually it was one with some sort of special markings. When Mom turned the baby chicks loose we would start looking for our favorite. It took me a long time to realize that the cute little black chicks with snippets of yellow would turn into barred adult chickens. So the chick you picked today for its markings would grow up to be like the other black and white birds.

Donny would always look for the "different". He got his wish. About this time one of the Banty hens appeared with two or three chicks. They looked like a Rhode Island Red - Bantam cross. Donny chose a rooster. A feisty pint sized bundle of attitude dressed in dark red feathers. Early on we knew this rooster was special. He survived a skunk attack that killed his siblings and also being locked out of the chicken house overnight.

When we went to do chores one morning there he sat on a lower branch of a tree looking both smug and belligerent at the same time. Donny blamed me for locking his rooster out. I thought this was the reason the silly red chicken turned mean. His overnight post became a favorite hangout from which he could swoop down on unsuspecting prey; dog, cats, kids or adults, no one was safe from the flash of red that would strike the unsuspecting with wings and beak to the heels.

Bare feet no matter how fast could not out run the little red demon. On a regular basis Mom or Dad would threaten the little beast with a trip to the cooking pot, with those threats Donny would fasten him in the chicken pen. However being the escape artist that he was that would only last a day or two. Donny made a "harness" of hay binder twine that fit around the body of the little red rooster. With this harness and a length of twine Donny could lead or at least get his pet to go in the general direction of where he wanted to go. As time passed you could see the two of them going about their business of strolling around the yard. Even stranger than the two walking together was the fact that the rooster never attacked Donny when he picked him up. He would try to peck me if I even looked at him.

Somehow the rooster could wander the hog pen, barn lot, pasture or even the road and never so much as lose a feather, so it was a real mystery when we got up one morning and found nothing but a few brilliant red feathers under his perch. The rooster had been free to run all day and had managed to avoid any of the attempts we made to catch him. When we came in from play after supper there he sat on his perch looking defiant, just daring little hands to try to put him in a pen. What happened in the night forever remained a mystery. Donny loved the little red fellow and did not take a baby chick for a pet ever again, that I can remember. However Donny moved on to bigger and tougher things like riding the large pigs and calves. Each year there was a new crop that came under his expert riding ability.

10

Family Night Out

Saturdays were special for our family, we took the cream and eggs to town to be sold, grocery shopped and the four of us kids went to see the latest western movie. We all looked forward to Saturdays. The eggs and cream were packed into the trunk of the car and Mom with her list of supplies in hand began herding the four of us kids into the car. As usual Donny had some last minute thing he was doing and would came hurling himself around the corner of the house when Mom called him using his full name. We settled in for the trip to town. As we backed out of the drive, I asked Donny "are you sure you shut the gate to the barn lot." "Yes, I shut the gate," was his defiant reply. The gate would close and lock but unless you put the bar through the iron slot and pushed it down the animals especially the cows could push against it and come through.

"Did you lock the gate," I asked?

Donny turned to me with a big frown on his face and said, "Yes, I shut the gate and I locked the gate, now leave me alone." And I did! With that he forgot all about the gate. I did not.

Donny was always in such a hurry to get from one place to another that he did not always finish one thing before starting something new. We had a brindle milk cow that was an expert at escaping. I thought she was ugly, big ears and big eyes, and a distain for little kids. Jerry sat on Moms lap but kept trying to peek into the back seat to see what Donny and Danny were doing. I rode herd on Danny and listened to Donny tell some wild story that Danny believed. Donny dwelled in his make believe world about as much as he did in the real world. He always had fun in which ever world he was in.

Our town had buildings on the north side of the main street, built into a hill. The sidewalk was several feet above the roadway. There was a solid wall of concrete next to the street. While my folks did their shopping the two little boys and I sat on the sidewalk, with our legs dangling over the side, eating ice cream cones as we watched the traffic on the street below. The drug store had the best ice cream and was right next to the place where Mom took her cream and eggs to sell. Donny and Dad were off to the hardware store, or feed store or wherever. Sometimes I envied Donny his freedom however I got into a lot less trouble. After Mom sold the cream and eggs and did her shopping, she stored the groceries in the trunk of the car. She would then buy movie tickets and almost always a western would be playing.

I would take the two little guys and sit between them down in the lower part of the theater. Donny always had to sit with the big guys. Sometimes the way Donny remembered the movies, I wondered if I had been in the same theater. After the movie Donny and I and several of our cousins would be there, we would all go to the end of the street where there would be musicians tuning up guitars, fiddles and sometimes a piano. They were getting ready to play for the square dancers. Mom and Dad and usually two or three of Moms brothers and their wives would be there. Uncle Charlie would call the dance and he always had a square dance set at the corner of the floor where he stood and he would instruct us kids. By the time the dance was over, everyone had about as much Saturday as they could stand. Most of the people were farmers and had already put in a full day's work. Dad and Mom would load four sleepy kids in the car and we would head for home.

As we pulled into our drive and Dad parked the car under the big old tree the headlights picked up two large shiny orbs. There on top of the root cellar eating the new grass Dad had replanted stood the big eared, big eyed brindle cow. Dad was not happy as he knew this cow did not go around anything she could walk over. Also she would have gone through the area where the small individual houses for the hens with baby chicks were, turning over feeders and water jars. Thank goodness the hens were shut in for the night. We all got out of the car and Mom carried Jerry who was asleep into the house. Dad started for the barn for a feed bucket to lure the cow back into the barn lot.

In a loud authoritative voice Donny said, "Well, Evelyn you didn't lock the gate again!" I wanted to pinch his silly little head off. But Mom and Dad were not fooled. After Dad got the cows back in, the other cows were in the south side of the yard, thank goodness there was a fence around Moms garden, and he had assessed the damage he gave Donny a good talking to and Donny found himself in big trouble with extra chores for a while.

On Saturday nights in the winter time my parents listened to the Grand Old Opry from Nashville Tennessee. The National Barn Dance from Chicago with such familiar names as Patsy Cline, Ernest Tubb, Eddy Arnold and Hank Williams. For me it might as well have been Mars. They would listen to the end of these programs when we got home from town in the summer.

✺

When we moved to Christian Forty we didn't have electricity or telephone. We lived at the end of the road and electric power stopped about a half mile from us. Until at least two other families moved in we would have to wait. The elderly gentleman that owned the house south of us didn't want that "electric stuff" in his house. We had a radio that was battery operated. We kids listened to our cowboy heroes that came on about as soon as we got home from school. Our radio sat on top of a box like cabinet that had no doors. The front and sides were solid wood with carved trim around each of the panels. The back was hollow with several shelves built in. I am guessing it was at least five foot wide and two foot deep. It was made of dark wood polished and varnished to a high gloss and stood about four foot high. Mom could pull it out away from the wall and that was where she stored her thread, sewing and her finished crochet pieces.

Sofa and chair sets, dresser sets and table cloths all made in the pineapple pattern were my favorites. People from other towns came and bought her work. Donny and I thought we had to be as close to the radio as we could get, almost in the midst of the action. As each program finished one could see the wheels in Donny's head grinding out the plot to fit us when we played cowboy. And I just lived to be the villain. It was that or I didn't get to play. It never occurred to me that if I didn't play the part Donny told me to, Donny would be a hero unto himself.

When it was time to go to bed the lingering story of the western or the mystery would remain. I would start the "what if" theory and sometimes have myself too scared to go to sleep and I was glad I shared a room with my little brothers. Jerry slept with me while Danny and Donny shared the other bed across the room. Just about the time I was scared enough to think about finding Mom to ask her to clarify my "what ifs" Donny would tell Danny some goofy story and they would start giggling. Mom would appear and hush them up. Jerry would be asleep by now, and the boogie man would sort of fade into the dark and somewhere in the timber the night birds would call. I could hear the soft breathing of my baby brother and somehow the world was so right.

The following day we would play out one of the western stories from the night before. We were good, we didn't have a script but we could put several stories together. We just made up things as we went along. No wonder it seldom worked out since the two of us were never on the same story.

Our favorite pastime was to act out our most recent trip to the movies. So this time with Donny as the bad guy, (he always got to be tough) and I was the good guy (always turned the other cheek) we got on our horses and reenacted the chase, capture and the ride into the sun set.

On this particular occasion I was the sheriff and Donny was the outlaw. He was using the saddle which he did sometimes when riding Lady, I preferred to ride bareback so there were no fights at this time over the saddle. I was supposed to walk up to him sitting on his horse and just like in the movies I was about to arrest him. In this one particular scene the bad guy escaped by kicking the Sheriff in the jaw and galloping off. Everything went fine till we reached the kicking part. I had threatened his life and limbs if he really did kick me! Donny assured me his foot would go past my head and at that point I should fall back and pretend to be unconscious.

The plan was good but the stirrup was too wide. The edge of the stirrup struck me across the left eyebrow. Blood gushed over my face, neck and hands. I howled The Banshee scream for Mom and I left my horse standing and ran to the house. It seemed the horses were never surprised at what we did. Donny wandered in and gave me as much sympathy as he could muster, then suggested we try it again! My head hurt too much to answer him. Later I was not pleased with my black eye, but off he went with his silly cow-lick sticking up like an antenna for trouble.

⚬⚬⚬

Some of the things we saw at the movies were definitely not meant to be tried at home. Donny had a knack for making some of his ideas actually seem possible but his idea of how to mount his horse a new way was sure not for me.

The guy in the movie jumped off a porch roof onto his horse and rode away. This looked easy enough to Donny. He informed me that he was going to jump out of the hay loft onto Lady, ride off to the west part of the pasture where I was to run him down and arrest him. This was going to be something different. As I sat on my horse Billy right off I could see several things wrong with the plan. One that the hay loft door looked a long way down to the ground and how was he going to keep the horse there without tying her, and there was no chance of me catching Donny and Lady when I was riding Billy. Donny assured me he had it all planned out. That should have been a clue.

His plan was that he would feed Lady to keep her standing and he proceeded to push a bale of hay out of the loft. He brought Lady below the loft door and when he was satisfied that she couldn't resist the hay he raced into the barn and up the ladder to the loft. He appeared at the door of the hay loft all smiles and cow-lick then he disappeared. The next thing I heard was the sound of bare feet running across the loft floor. Billy and I were well out of the way because the action was about to begin. Donny flew out of the hay loft feet first straight for his horse. Lady did one of her quick side steps without so much as missing a bite. Donny landed feet and butt first in the hay pile, eye to eye with his getaway horse. It seemed Lady was never surprised at anything Donny did.

He was one fortunate kid, if he had landed astride of the horse he would have sang soprano forever. The other problem was he was facing north when he came out of the loft and his getaway horse was facing south. He would have been riding backward, and I don't think Lady was so inclined to do circus tricks. We turned the horses loose and retired to the front yard to regroup. Thoughtfully Donny climbed his tree to think out another plan. Donny had a sore ankle for a few days but that only gave him more time to refine his next escapade. This was one time my common sense won out over idiocy.

⁓⊙⊙⁓

Like all kids everywhere Donny and I would rather play than do chores. In our case we would choose to ride our horses. The western movies we saw on Saturday night were filled with adventure and would last the week long for us to play out the story. We would play our western hero movie lines, sometimes too real. For most of the time it was so much more fun to act out the movies or make up our own stories than to do chores. Donny and I decided that we would just run away from home and be cowboys. Mom had told us to help hoe the garden and as everyone knows that is a dull boring job. You really have to pay attention otherwise you get weeds and vegetables mixed and cut it all down which would cause "Mother Wrath" to come down on you.

We never had too many chores but we were expected to do them correctly.

It was late afternoon when we informed Mom of our intensions to leave home and hearth and venture out into the world to become cowboys even if we had no cows to herd, and we would have been in real trouble had we been silly enough to herd our milk cows. Of course she asked us where we were going, since we were not allowed to go past the mailbox a mile to the north. She also wanted to know how we would feed ourselves and our horses, which by the way we were taking with us, and no we hadn't asked if we could take them. What is a cowboy without a horse? As we told her we were expecting the neighbors to just fall all over one another to get to feed us and our horses, she looked appropriately sad and dismayed at our announcement.

We told her we were going to scout out a campsite. We would be back later to pick up our "gear" we were now in old west mode and living it up. We galloped off to the far side of the orchard where we each found a good campsite (but not too far apart). No sharing a fireless space for these two rough and ready cowboys besides we were not allowed to touch matches.

As we returned home Donny was proud of himself that he had made this decision (and of course had allowed me to come along) in time to get out of doing the evening chores. We made the turn into our drive and there sat three grocery bags full of our clothes and toys! Mom came out of the cellar with the milk buckets followed by Danny and Jerry. I suspect she had been watching for our return from this advantage point. She wished us luck on our adventure and told us that IF we were ever back in this part of the country again that we could stop in for Sunday dinner, if they were home. With that little speech she and the two little boys headed to the barn to do the milking. She had to drag Danny along as he wanted to join us.

"Sunday dinner?" we had not even planned for tonight's supper. We sat our horses dumbfounded. I was the first to have second thoughts as the sun was getting low to the west and told Donny so. In unison we jumped off our horses and turned them loose in the barn lot. Next we carried our "gear" into the house and made a run for the barn. Mom was milking one of several cows to be milked, humming a familiar tune while Danny and Jerry played in the corn crib where she could watch them.

Donny and I grabbed a milk bucket each, took our milk stools from their pegs and started our chores. If I had given it any thought I would have wondered why Mom took three buckets to the barn since the milk was never left to sit but was taken to the cellar after each cow was milked.

Later that evening at supper Mom sort of mentioned that she hoped there would be enough since she wasn't expecting Donny and me for supper. I had no comment but was sure glad to have supper and a bed to go to as it was black as pitch outside.

Donny on the other hand spun a yarn about having a lot of things he had to do before he could go, but he was sure Mom and Dad would miss him and be sad he was gone. I thought I glimpsed a smile cross Moms face. Funny, after that night there were no longer plans for the two of us to run away again. I simply wanted not part of that, although Donny always had big plans to do great things. I was happy roaming the apple orchard on my horse and didn't mind the chores I had to do.

Part III

11

A New Baby Arrives

On January 10, 1949 our baby sister Shirley Faye was born in the hospital in Taylorville. We were all excited as I was the only girl so I was particularly thrilled to have a baby sister. Dad's sister in law, Victoria Bell, whom we called Aunt Tory-Bell, was in the same hospital giving birth to twins. She and Mom were best of friends and they managed to see each other while they were there. The two of them had taken care of Dad's mother when she was ill until she passed away. Mom and Aunt Tory-Belle were closer than sisters.

From the time of Mom's delivery she hemorrhaged even when she got home. And it became worse. The Doctor that the coal mine company insisted all miner's family's use was really not even qualified to be a dog catcher let alone deliver a baby. Mom was very weak and as time went by she got to the point that she was unable to walk without assistance. The Doctor was called to the house several times where he packed Mom with gauze and would leave hardly saying anything to Mom or Dad.

That spring Dad tried to take care of our forty acres. He let all the rented farm land go. He didn't train any horses nor did he buy any Tennessee Jersey heifers. I spent less and less time outside and more time inside the house. There was so much to be done and I never seemed to get caught up.

During this time Shirley cried most of the time. Mom could not make enough milk to nurse her. She was put on a bottle within a short period of time after Mom became bed fast and she developed sores in her mouth called thrush. I was later told that I did not sterilize her bottles long enough. Mom was so weak she could seldom do more than sit in a chair while Dad and I changed her bed. She was losing so much weight. I was staying home from school most of the time now to care for the baby and Mom. Dad still worked nights so there was no way he could leave a five year old, a newborn and a sick wife even for a short time.

Dad would do the laundry and I hung it up and took it down. Dad did the cooking now and started teaching me how to cook. I realized that I loved to bake, and we had cakes often, I tried to fix things Mom liked since she ate very little. I had a terrible time staying off my horse. I felt like a caged bird, I knew I had things to do cooking and cleaning but I was thirteen and house bound. I would put potatoes on to cook and go for a "short" ride only to come back and the potatoes were scorched or burned. I wanted my horse Billy in the lot closest to the house. I believe Mom and Dad knew how hard it was for me as they never got angry or made me turn the horse loose. I had to learn that lesson myself.

The Doctor came a few more times telling Dad she was getting better but even I could see she was becoming increasingly worse. Finally one night she lost conscious. By this time Dad and the daughter of the neighbor south of us and the neighbors to the north had managed to get the telephone company to bring the lines to the houses. Thank God they did as I had to call Dad home from the coal mine at least two times. One thing I never understood was where were all the folks Mom had fed huge dinners to? Sisters and sisters-in-law were scarce. On two separate occasions one sister in law came to the house, looked things over and told me I was not keeping house like Mom did. No help just advice.

And then the night came when Mom passed out and smelling salts could not revive her. I called the mine phone several times but there was no answer. The telephone in the mine was at a central location and whoever was near answered it. It could be a long period of time from when a call was placed until the miner got the message especially if the miner was in the tunnel. The call would sit on a note board until he checked it. Mom's brothers and two brothers-in-law were supposed to check for Dad but they were not always working in the same tunnel. I left several messages. I let the little boys think Mom was asleep they were so good and quiet. I had to tell Donny, he knew something was very wrong.

By about six or seven pm and I still had no word from Dad I called Mom and Dad Richards home and Aunt Vesta answered. I told her what was going on and by now I was crying and having difficulty talking. I told her Mom kept passing out for longer periods of time. I told her I had tried to call Dad but couldn't get a message to him. I asked her to please come to us, I was so scared. Aunt Vesta suggested that I should try to call some of the other family that she had a date and had to hang up she was already late! Instead of calling anyone else I waited until Dad came home when he got my message. Mom and Dad Richards didn't come either. I became angry and bitter until I felt I was wearing an albatross around my neck and I it remained for quite some time. It took many years for me to work through that experience and forgive Vesta and my grandparents. I was angry and Aunt Gerry talked to me about it. In later years I realized it was not for their sake she wanted me to forgive but for my own sake and peace of mind.

⌒◎⌒

This period of time was dark but would become darker. The Doctor for the coal mine could not be persuaded to let Dad take Mom to the hospital. I have never seen my Dad so angry. On one occasion the doctor told Mom and Dad to make certain that I washed my hands very good after I handled the bloody sheets or bed pads. I believe he knew Mom had cancer and did not know how to treat it other than packing her and refused to give up his pay for treating her.

From her bed Mom taught me to cook more than breakfast type food. It was hard for me to give up my horse for the kitchen. I was thirteen years old and could harness and work a team in the fields with Dad and Donny. There were times that Donny and I both had to work together to get a one person job done. But I didn't know much about cooking.

Dad broke with the coal mine rules and Doctor and took Mom to Memorial Hospital in Springfield. Mom's sister Sina and Uncle Frank went to the hospital to ask Mom and Dad if they could take care of the baby while she was in the hospital. Shirley was sick and could not eat and the mine doctor told us we had to "make" her take her bottle. Aunt Sina and Uncle Frank took Shirley and all her things and it was so sad to see the little baby leaving and it left all of us crying. Dad explained that we needed help with her or she might die. Aunt Sina took her to a Doctor who said the baby had thrush. She had sores in her mouth which were caused because I had not boiled or sterilized her bottles long enough.

The day Mom went to the hospital was March 14, Jerry's sixth birthday. When Dad left he said he did not know when he would be home but that he would stay with Mom as long as it took to get help. He told me to take care of the little boys and for Donny to help me. It was early morning when they left.

In the two months from when her baby was born to the present time Mom had gone from a healthy vibrant five foot eleven inch woman to a silent hollow-eyed skeletal person we children could hardly recognize. There was no laughter in our home now. None of the family on either side of the house offered to help us after Dad called all the family to keep them informed of Mom's tests.

Dad had sold some of the hogs and some of the cows, so we had fewer chores to do. We had the horses and Mom's chicken's ducks and geese to feed. We did not put out any garden in the spring nor did Dad have the means or time to try to plant any crops. That was the first of long nights to come. I guess I thought that when Dad came home he would bring Mom, and she would be alright. Two days later Dad came home, alone. I had never seen my Dad cry or look so forlorn. My parents had always preached truth and I asked if Mom was going to be alright. It took a while for him to answer and he said he sure hoped so. He said that several Doctors had seen Mom and she would have to stay in the hospital for a long time.

I believe Mom knew she was dying. During the last weeks she was home, as she grew weaker she spent so much time talking to me about growing up, how I was supposed to act and what was really important in life. She would repeat the lessons until they were burned into my brain. Things like honesty, loyalty and the love of family and God. She told me to take care of myself, to respect my body and not allow anyone to touch me in a sexual way, (and she was very explicit,) until I got married.

Each morning as early as Dad could get chores done he would leave and go to the hospital, getting home in time to go to work. I was staying home with Jerry now, there did not seem to be anyone who would help with his care. Finally Dad told Donny and me that Mom had a disease called cancer. He said he did not know how long it would take for her to get well. We wanted to see her so badly but the hospital had rules and kids were not allowed in. Later I learned from an aunt that Mom had surgery, xray treatments and radiation in an attempt to stop the uterine cancer.

When it became clear that Mom would be gone for a long while, Dad's mine foreman Fred Patton stepped up and helped Dad keep his job. The mine wanted to fire him for taking Mom to Springfield. The mine said they would not pay for her hospital or doctor bills.

That spring Dad began to sell the remainder of the livestock, I did not mind when the hogs were sold but it broke my heart when the cows and horses were sold. The first to go was his beloved Percherons; they were worth the most, then the milk cows that took the most time, keeping only one cow for our use. He kept Mom's chickens and sold the rest of the fowl. Finally the only horses we had was Billy and Lady Molly and Queen, I believe Dad knew that we would have to have something to hold onto in order to start over when Mom got home. I don't think he ever gave up that Mom would not recover.

Mom was having a hard time being away from her children but the hospital had rules that children under the age of fourteen could not visit a patient in the hospital. However she persuaded the Doctors to let her come home for a visit. The weather was warm now for June and Dad got a lounge chair and placed it in the front yard. She wanted to be outside so badly. We were so happy to see Mom but I hardly recognized her, she was so thin, and her beautiful hair was almost totally grey. She could only stay during the day then Dad had to take her back, it was a Sunday and we kids rode back to the hospital with them. I had seen the hospital from the outside since Dad took us each Saturday and Sunday when he went to visit but to see a wheelchair come and get my Mom was ominous.

One of the most vivid memories I have is of Mom' sister Rosie and some friends came and picked the cherries. That was the only time she ever came to our home that I know of. Later when the peaches and grapes were ripe they all disappeared while we were gone. The fruit left our place but nothing ever came back in the form of finished pies or cobblers. Perhaps my folks gave someone permission to take the fruit I don't know but Dad didn't act like it. But what did I know I was thirteen years old.

Her last visit home was late July and she could stay overnight. Dad put a roast in the oven and I baked enough for the week end so I could be near Mom. The little guys were so good and kept themselves clean in their Sunday clothes they were starting to outgrow. Mom made a fuss about how tall they were getting which pleased them so much, she mentioned how strong Donny was getting. I didn't understand why she cried and held me. Although I was already tall and strong, and she could not tell me I was pretty and keep a straight face. I didn't know why she was crying.

After dinner Dad took the boys with him to the grocery store in town. Mom said she needed to talk to me. She told me how I was to respect my body and never let anyone touch me if I felt uncomfortable. I wondered about this talk since she had told me this several times. She told me I must go to school as long as I could and learn as much as I could learn. Then she told me something that turned my blood cold. She said IF she did not get well and passed away she was giving me two of her precious babies, Danny and Jerry, for me to care for. She said I was to care for them as she had cared for me. I realized that I had to put the little guys first always. Danny would soon be eight and Jerry was six. I was confused and overwhelmed but Mom said God would guide me all I had to do was ask for His help.

She said she and Dad had told Aunt Sina and Uncle Frank that they could raise Shirley. Dad and the boys came home and she said we would talk the next day. She looked so tired, and Dad wanted her to go into the house to her bed but she said she wanted to stay outside longer. Dad sent Donny to feed the horses and I went to finish supper. Dad carried her inside before the air chilled and went to milk the one cow we had.

Dad remarked that she ate a good supper, better than she ate in the hospital and I was so pleased when she told me what a good meal I had prepared. But she couldn't keep the food in her stomach. It was about 6 pm when Dad went to check the stock as he did every night after he got home from work. He ran back to the house and told the little boys to stay with Mom and for me to get my jeans on and for Donny and me to go with him. Mom knew something was wrong and made Dad tell her. All he said was "its Billy." Mom knew immediately what had happened as we had been through this before. As loveable as he was Billy had a bad habit of gobbling down his grain. Dad kept golf ball sized rocks in Billy's feed box to slow down his eating. We never fed him oats alone but mixed his feed with shelled corn. Donny in his hurry to feed the stock had grained the horses but forgot to mix shelled corn for Billy.

When Dad heard him coughing he knew what was wrong. Dad put a halter on Billy not a bridle and gave me a leg up, telling me to run him as hard as I could so he would cough and break up the ball of oats lodged in his throat. I did just that, Donny was on Lady and we set off riding hard in the pasture. Billy coughed up the oats and he and I were both wringing wet with sweat. Donny took Billy and walked the horses until they cooled off. Dad did not let the horses drink water until later that evening. He kept Billy in the barn all night, and he checked on him before going to bed. It was good to hear his greeting whicker. Everything looked fine but he developed a cough and two or three days later my horse Billy died of pneumonia.

⁓ɔ⍨

From the time that Uncle Fred and Aunt Gerry Patton (they were no relation whatsoever, but became our angels in time of need) became aware of our desperate situation they helped us. Aunt Gerry now kept all four of us till Dad got home from work. Donny Danny and I rode the bus to and from school and back home, we did what chores we had to do and Aunt Gerry would come out and get us and take us to her house for supper help me bathe the two little guys put them down on pallets and she would help Donny and me do our homework. She did this until school ended. Dad rode to work with Uncle Pat and he would gather his brood and take us home around midnight. These two people who were no relation to us at all saved Dad's sanity, he left Jerry with them while he went to see Mom, and took her our letters and drawings, which Aunt Gerry encouraged us to do.

We did not put out any garden in the spring nor did Dad have the means or time to try to plant any crops. One of the most vivid memories I have is of Mom's sister Rosie and a couple of her friends coming and picking the cherries, then the peaches and apples but there was never a pie in return, and that was the only time they came to our home. Mom Richards never came. The family was blaming Dad for Mom's impending death, and there was no forgiveness. The Doctors allowed Mom to be wheeled to a waiting room so she could see her children. She never got to come home again.

When I became older I learned much of the Richards family that I did not like. There had been an arranged marriage of sorts between Mom's parents and an older man, who according to Aunt Lena was wealthy. The family believed Mom had married a bad bargain in my

Dad. They never forgave her. For one thing many years later they seemed to remember "helping" us but could not name anything specific. In fact they seldom came around except to criticize.

On August 16th Mom passed away. We were at Aunt Gerry's when Mom's niece Ellen came and got us. This was very unusual since none of the family had paid any attention to us. Aunt Gerry said it was Ok for us to go. I don't think Aunt Gerry knew Mom was gone, she knew that Dad was at the hospital and Mom's family certainly was not going to give up any information. Later that evening Ellen told us that Mom was gone. We four kids were sitting on the stairs when we were told of Moms death. We stayed there until Dad came and got us. We were at a total loss. The next three days were a blur. Aunt Gerry and Dad bought clothes for us for the funeral. Mom was buried on a Friday. Uncle Ray's body had been returned from Germany two or three days before Mom's funeral. Four years after he was killed he was buried the Sunday after Mom's funeral on Friday. I have no doubt that it was hard on the Richards family however Aunt Vesta found the strength to torment Uncle Ray's wife Josephine about the same way she did my Dad, with lies, there was no truth in the woman.

At Mom's funeral Vesta had her hysterical fit but this time Dad called her on it. I have no idea what he said to her but the small church became quiet with subdued sobs. After Dad returned to where we were sitting I could hear murmurs over where Vesta, Mom and Dad Richards were sitting. I had a terrible premonition that there would be trouble and I was right. It wasn't that I was so smart just that I was an observer of people. Vesta was the youngest of ten children and she was so spoilt that her every whim, cry or commotion was cause for alarm. Vesta was a born trouble maker who had to have constant attention. She had caused terrible problems with her siblings and their spouses. Mom had taken her to task for her despicable treatment of Uncle Rays wife Aunt Josephine when he joined the Army.

I feared Vesta because I knew that Dad would not put up with her nonsense. He was angry because she wouldn't go to Mom when Mom needed her so badly. She did what she was best at, causing trouble. She started lies concerning Dad and other women, she "couldn't remember their names" and that my Dad was a drunkard. This was a bald faced lie as Dad could account for his day minute by minute. Dad drank more now but I never saw him drunk.

Jerry became ill and was diagnosed with rhemautic fever soon after Mom came home the last time. It took Dad and me to take care of him as he was too weak to walk and had to be helped up and down. Dad moved a day bed into the living room for Jerry and I slept on the couch because we were up so much in the night. When Jerry could not sleep I read to him until he dozed off. Dad had to have sleep he was about done in from months of trying to do everything himself, so Jerry was my responsibility.

❧❦❧

When school started that fall all four of us went on the bus. Jerry still had to take medicine but he was getting well. I took my job of caring for the little boys serious and I became fourteen on the 4th of September and was in the eighth grade. Jerry became so insecure after Mom died that he became upset when I was away from him. We rode the school bus into town and I saw fear in his eyes. Danny and Donny thought the bus was fun. Danny did not protest very much when I made him sit near me. Donny was a different matter. One morning in his haste to be first on the bus Donny tripped and hit his face on the top step. He wasn't really hurt but he broke one of his front teeth. Now he had one more "badge" to join his scars.

I had often wondered how it was that I was taller than Donny and had much longer legs but he could run faster than me until one day it dawned on me that what Donny did best was run. He ran even if he was just crossing the room. I thought if that's what it takes to catch up with him I can do that. So I started to run and run and run. The more I ran the better I liked it and this habit proved very useful.

The bus let the little kids off at the grade school first. Donny and I were in the eighth grade and our classes were at the high school. I would get off the bus with Danny and Jerry. Danny had no problem going to his class, Donny had coached him. Jerry was a different matter. He cried when I left him, he was so afraid that I wouldn't be there for him after school. I stayed in his room until the class started, then I would slip out of the room. The teacher said that he was ok after a while. I would run from the grade school across the yard of the adjoining church where Mom's funeral had been (and I believe that had something to do with Jerry's fear of loss he saw that church every time he was outside) across the highway and to the gym where school had started. Almost always the bell would have rung so I was considered late. As can be expected I got into trouble. If I had only told someone why I was late but I had become a "do it myself person" so I never explained nor told anyone. The school sent notes to Dad by way of me but I never gave them to him.

Finally the school principal watched a few days to see why I wasn't on the bus and why was I late. I was called into Mr. Randles office and much to my surprise he told me I was not to go into the gym by the main door but to go to the side door where the school would not be aware of my coming in. I was very grateful to the principal and the teachers for their help. I wasn't a good student but I was getting passing grades, the classes were hard since I had missed so much school the year before. I still had to really work hard to keep up at school, with the little boys and housework. The teachers went out of their way to help me, and I could do some of the work on the weekends, with Dad's help.

Dad was doing everything he could to keep his debts paid but nothing worked. He had sold all the stock except one cow and a few chickens. All the machinery he and Uncle Buck had worked so hard to repair was sold. He had to sell everything we could do without, even the big cook stove in the summer kitchen along with the big table and chairs and the canners and big butchering kettles we would no longer ever use. The hospital bills were overwhelming and now Dad was getting threatening letters. At one point in time I saw a hospital bill with so many numbers that I couldn't read it.

∽∂∾

When Mom was buried in the Edinburg cemetery I could not get the reason off my mind. I knew Dad had bought a six grave plot at Southfork cemetery and that was where Baby Carold was buried. Mom had planted a pink Peony bush on his grave. So why was Mom not buried with her baby? Finally I could not stand it any longer and I asked Dad why? Dad told me that Mom and Dad Richards had paid for Mom's funeral and that Vesta had a hissy fit, insisting Mom be buried at Edinburg, she got her way and Mom was buried at Edinburg. I was sure perfecting my hate. Vesta could not separate my parents in life so the vindictive person she was got the job done in death. My parents weren't the only family Vesta tormented, Uncle Charlie, Aunt Emma and Uncle Jim all had seen her wrath.

One of the most ridiculous things she told anyone she talked to was that two weeks before Shirley was born Dad had made Mom help bale hay! Shirley was born the 10th of January six months after hay baling and Dad always had balers help him, Mom cooked.

The winter after Mom died Dad found a baby sitter for us. He was Aunt Lena's dad and he did light kitchen work he was a crippled man, and all Dad wanted him to do was see to it there was a warm house for us to come home from school to because Dad was afraid of fires. He cooked light meals for us and he would go home before we went to bed at eight p.m. When Dad got home from work he would wake Donny and me to find out how the day went and careful to ask if there was anything he needed to know. He helped to keep Donny under control. We didn't get any help from the family but we got lots of advice.

∽∂∾

One evening not long after Mom died two of Moms sisters and some other women came to our house and took all of Moms crocheted pieces. There was an arm load of finished work. Dad had not been able to bring himself to sell them and my aunts just took everything. I had one small piece from the top of my dresser for a keepsake.

Different folks would show up unexpected after school, Saturday, Sunday to give us "instructions." One aunt informed Dad and me that we were not keeping house the way Mom did. However again she didn't offer to help.

We saw very little of Shirley Faye from the time Aunt Sina and Uncle Frank took her when she was so ill. Now she was a happy baby and very much loved but we just didn't get to see her often. She always wore such beautiful dresses and she was so sweet. We didn't get to hold her.

✍◦◎

On March 13, 1950 Uncle Buck was killed in a coal mine accident. Dad and Uncle Buck worked with Uncle Frank, and Dad and Uncle Buck were riding on the coal car when it took a curve fast and Uncle Buck hit the wall. This was something that jolted Dad again, as Uncle Buck was a close friend to my Dad. Sometimes I would wake up and find my Dad drinking coffee and smoking cigarettes at the kitchen table in the early hours of the morning. I believed that is what he was living on, he ate very little.

Donny was getting harder to control. He of course did not want to take orders from a sister that was only fourteen months older than he was. The rural schools had consolidated and we all went to town school. Donny and Alfred continued to fight at the school in town, which gave substance to the idea "bring those country kids in here and there will be trouble." As fate would have it both families rode the same school bus. Helen and I tried to keep the peace between the boys. Danny and Jerry watched Donny and his antics with much interest. One of my fears was that the two little boys would start doing some of the things they saw the older boys doing. Heaven forbid!

✍◦◎

One evening on the way home from school, Donny got into a fight on the school bus. Donny always sat in the back of the bus with the big kids. I made Danny and Jerry sit with me. I don't know who the fight was with since the bus picked up kids we didn't know. I also didn't know what the fight was about. But suddenly the bus made a sudden stop and the driver ordered Donny off the bus. Donny marched past my seat head high and angry.

Before I knew what was happening Danny followed Donny and Jerry followed Danny. I yelled at them to come back but it was too late. They got off the bus right behind Donny. I gathered jackets, books and papers, I usually did my reading homework on the bus and I too got off. I thought the two little boys were too little to walk the two miles home alone or with Donny's influence. When I caught up with Donny I ranted and yelled at him all the way home. Donny later said he wished he had never gotten into the fight, because he was sick of my scolding him all the way home. But that was nothing to what happened when Dad found out. His theory was if we got into trouble at school we were in trouble at home.

One day while we were in town one of Moms brothers approached Dad soon after Mom died. He told Dad it would be best for his children if someone else took them. My Dad was speechless. My uncle said he knew a couple that wanted the two little boys and he would be glad to take them to his friends, they did not want us two older kids. My uncle knew that my Dad had promised Mom on her death bed that he would keep the family together. Also she had given the two little guys to me! She had made her wishes well known for what I believe she knew the fight Dad would have to keep us together. She knew her family very well. She would have been appalled at the very idea of splitting us up.

Dad stood silent for several minutes staring at my uncle. My uncle believed Dad had a losing battle but he didn't know my Dad. Dad then pulled himself up to his six foot three inch height and I was afraid he was going to hit my uncle. Instead he turned lose all the pent up frustration and anger that had built over the past months. My uncle soon backed down and he was by no means a little person of stature. Dads back was to the wall and the thought of losing his children and his promise to Mom was more than he could handle. I believe he also knew that the Richards clan would not stop and his only ally had been Uncle Buck. Now there was no one on his side in the Richards family. My uncle walked away from my Dad not saying a word, but Dad knew it was not over.

The day came when Dad sat us kids down at the kitchen table and told us we were going to have to move from Christian Forty. Dad was in debt to the hospital and doctors and the bank was foreclosing on the forty acres my parents were buying. Before Mom got sick we did not have to buy much of anything, she canned and preserved our fruits and vegetables. She made our own bread and baked goods and she made almost all of the clothes for us kids. Now Dad had to feed and clothe four kids and still meet all the other payments. It could not be done. All of us cried and begged to stay where we had so much joy and love. It was like losing Mom all over again but we prepared to move.

Sadly we packed up and moved to a rental house five or six miles east of town. Our new home was cold even that summer. I was so lonely, when we had been gone to town or somewhere I would pray that Mom would be there when we got home, although I knew it could not be. At our old home we were surrounded by the orchards barns and gardens. Now we were perched on top of a hill, it felt so vulnerable. We were safe at the end of the road at Christian Forty but at the new place we were just out in the open. We felt that thunderstorms were right on top of us. In our old home I never once felt scared but I was now, I knew I had to pretend I wasn't afraid because Danny and Jerry were afraid. I don't know if Donny was afraid or not who knew what he was thinking. Dad suggested that in the evening I make popcorn and the four of us play team checkers. We didn't know the rules for team checkers but Dad set down the rules and we had fun. The school bus stopped at our door and eventually we settled in.

Donny was still Donny and one day the boys were chasing one another through the house. I was doing laundry in the building just off the back porch. I had told the boys to stop running through the house, they didn't and I got after Donny with a broom. His last trip through he tripped over the rocker of the rocking chair and fell against the screen door and out onto the concrete stoop at the front door. Three neighboring high school kids were driving past and saw him fall. They stopped and said his shoulder might be broken. I asked them to take us to the Doctor in town but his office was closed. They took us to the coal mine Doctor whose office was in Kincaid.

The doctor walked into the room and asked which one was Donald. If he had looked he could see how white Donny's face was besides his shoulder stuck up on one side. He told Donny to come to the door and had Donny step up on a two step stool. He took Donny's left hand and put it up on top of the door and holding Donny's hand in place he put his entire weight on Donny's shoulder and pushed down. Donny fainted and slid to the floor. The Doctor stepped past him into another room and came back with an envelope with some white pills in it. He told us that was all and left the room no sling and heaven forbid not a word of sympathy to the child. The high school kids helped Donny back to the car. He was in a lot of pain but did not say a word he wouldn't have wanted anyone to think he wasn't tough. The high school kids were livid with anger at the doctor.

When we got home he took some of the pills as directed on the envelope and went to sleep. I was up when Dad got home from work. He was angry at the doctor for not putting Donny's arm in a sling. Dad used a dish towel and made a sling to keep him from moving his shoulder. Dad brought a sling home from the mine and it really helped. In a matter of days Donny was up and about again. His accident seemed to trigger more crazy stunts that were serious. It was if he had a death wish.

Dad had told the boys they had to help me do housework, the dishes and cleaning their rooms. Once when they were doing the dishes Donny for whatever reason attempted to stick a butcher knife into a wall. His hand slid down the knife and cut deep into the flesh at the base of his thumb. Wide eyed Jerry came and got me in the wash house. When I got to the kitchen there was blood everywhere. I didn't know what to do but Donny said he did. He had me tie a bandage very tight around his hand and told me how to make a tourniquet on his arm. It slowed the bleeding down. When Dad got home at midnight from second shift he said Donny needed stitches in his hand, so early the next morning he took Donny to the doctor in town to have his hand stitched.

❧❧

Donny discovered fish and frogs in the creek that made a half circle in back of our house. The boys caught fish and Dad taught them how to clean them. We put the fish in the freezer of the refrigerator until there was enough for a meal. Dad then taught me how to cook the fish to a crisp golden brown. The fish were a treat. Someone told Donny that frog legs were good to eat. He put great effort into catching frogs. He brought several to the house for me to cook. I knew absolutely nothing about cooking frogs but watched Donny as he proceeded to make a total mess of the kitchen. The last straw was when the legs began to flop out of the skillet and fling grease all over the stove. The boy's ate the frog legs and pronounced them delicious but they looked either raw or burned. I wanted no part of the things so I cleaned the stove and kitchen while the boys ate. After that they built a small fire at the creek and using an iron skillet they fried their catch of frog legs outdoors.

❧❧

We learned in school that peanuts were grown in the sandy soil in the southern United States. Being the ever enterprising person that Donny was he wanted to plant peanuts, Dad bought some raw peanuts and Donny soaked the peanuts in water overnight. The boys worked up the ground of a sandbar on the creek and Dad told them about where to plant their crop. Donny kept a note book on his project as he was going to use this as a school project.

All summer long the boys watched their crop. We woke up one morning to find frost on the grass and what few green leaves on the peanuts were black. It was time to dig the peanuts. Donny had learned how to roast them and set about putting his peanuts in the oven. Ever the skeptic I figured it would be another mess to clean up. Imagine my surprise when the peanuts all toasty hot and with salt on them were delicious. And I thought peanuts only came in little bags. Donny had succeeded in his project and took some of the results to school. Not an A student he was well pleased with his grade, but that was the last of his farming adventures.

❦

The boys were getting older and were more prone to mischief, especially with Donny's guidance. I knew I would have a really hard summer, there was no controlling Donny and Danny and Jerry wanted to go and do whatever he did. I had to get used to seeing "Don" (he got rid of the "baby" name) climbing over, hanging from or digging under but always on the move.

One of my pet peeves was running in the house. They would chase one another and wrestle, all of which I did not like. I heard the back porch screen door slam several times, but I had my hands full doing laundry which it seemed I never got finished with. I ignored the slamming door until suddenly the Banshee scream split the air and I ran to see what had happened now. Danny was sitting on the porch floor near the door holding his foot. As he was running to the door his foot slid on the wooden porch floor and drove a wide piece of wood into the sole of his foot. There was no blood just that piece of wood in his foot that I couldn't pull out. I knew it had to come out so I could clean it. I told Danny what I had to do and he just stared at me in disbelief, also I believe he was in shock.

I got bandages, and a new razor blade from Dad's shaving drawer. When I got back to Danny he was deathly white but he gritted his teeth and said nothing. I got the kerosene can washed my hands and his foot. Next I began to split the skin over the piece of wood in his foot, and it caused me to be sick to my stomach and have nightmares for a long time. I lifted the wood out, now there was blood, and a lot of it. I washed the wound with kerosene which I know burned but Danny did not say a word as I bandaged his foot. Danny then passed out and the fear on Jerry's face was heartbreaking. Donny helped me carry Danny to the sofa in the living room. No one said anything we were all too scared to talk. Danny woke up but didn't say anything, he was so still. I packed more bandages on top of the first to stem the blood flow. Danny told me it didn't hurt but I am certain it did. I slept on the floor by the sofa but he never said anything. When Dad got home from work he removed the bandages to be sure this was a clean wound and said it looked pretty good. We kept Danny in bed for a few days but not for long. Don made him a cane and by walking on his heel he was up and going everywhere.

Part IV

12

High School

I was a freshman in high school that next fall and it was so difficult for me. I had so much trouble with Algebra while Don breezed through with no problem. I would do my schoolwork after the boys went to bed as I had to help Danny and Jerry with their homework. When I got flustered and simply could not figure out the algebra problems I would wake Don to ask for help. Being awakened from a sound sleep to help me with my homework did not sit well with him. He would march to the kitchen table his cowlick sticking up, write out the answer and with a glare return back to his bed. He never explained how he arrived at the answers. Finally my teacher Mr. Anselm talked to me and said he didn't want to fail me and had talked to the home economics teacher, they believed it would be to my benefit for me to drop algebra and take an extra class of home economics. Dad agreed to the suggestion and I was very happy. I got to take an advanced sewing course because Mom had taught me the basics.

We put out a garden and with the advice from my teacher I began to can simple vegetables since Dad had kept one of Mom's small canners. I learned to love to work in the garden but didn't have time to do much, Dad and the boys did the garden work.

The freshman class was abuzz with plans for the spring-dance. Everyone was talking about what they were going to wear. I had no intentions of going as one of the "click girls" had already told me I couldn't bring "my babies" with me and if Danny and Jerry couldn't go I wouldn't go. Dad had received a letter from the school outlining the rules for the students as well as the acceptable time for arrival and leaving.

Dad talked to me about going and I told him I didn't want to go. I thought that was the end of it. Not so. Aunt Gerry had us come to her house after school one afternoon, not unusual, she sometimes fixed supper for us, a real treat. We only had a baby sitter at the old place for the winter after Mom died. We took care of ourselves now. She had a lime green formal for me to try on. It would need some alterations she said but declared it could be done. It really was a pretty dress and I had never tried on a formal before, I really kind of liked it. It looked like I was going to a dance. She also said she would talk to the school about the little boys since I simply refused not to go if they did not come with me. Since Don and I were in the same grade he would be going and would have to wear a white shirt and tie, not to his liking.

The night of the dance all of us were to go to Aunt Gerry's home after school. She washed my hair and I had my first bubble bath. She curled my long hair I guess braids were not appropriate and put a bit of makeup on me. I did feel pretty until I went into the living room and Don burst out laughing. I wanted to pinch his silly head off! Aunt Gerry had pulled some strings and all four of us went to the dance. We were all excited as Aunt Gerry dropped us off at the school gym. She would pick us up after the dance.

The inside of the gym had been transformed from a basketball court to streamers and tables of food. We met a couple of my classmates and got some food from the table. Don had gone off with his friends and I saw him sitting on the other side of the gym and for once he was acting like a gentleman.

I was asked to dance but since I did not know how I quietly refused. I was so tall, taller than any of my classmates and I felt so self-conscious. My friend Patsy P. didn't know how to dance either, so we were happy to sit on the bleachers and just watch. I remember how Danny and Jerry's eyes shone. They were happy.

Right on time Aunt Gerry picked us up and took us back to her house to sleep until Dad got back from work. For one magical evening I was like the other girls in my class, almost. I was the only girl with two little boys with her and I wasn't sorry for a minute. As for Danny and Jerry I will bet they were the only little kids in the county their age that went to a Spring Dance.

❦

I was fifteen when I became a woman and mention this only because nursing Mom with cancer I was positive I had cancer. I told no one and eventually my nerves gave way to the point of a break down. I began crying and couldn't stop. At wits end Dad took me to the doctor in town (not the mine doctor I wanted no part of the coal mine doctor) he talked to me for a long time asking personal questions and I had my first physical examination. Finally I told him of my fears and that I was failing Mom in my promise to take care of the two little boys. I will never forget the doctor jumping up and hugging me. He explained that what was happening to me was natural and would continue each month for the rest of my life until I was no longer child bearing age at about forty years old, which to me seemed like a forever in the future age. He called Dad in and told him to take me to a female relative to help me. The doctor gave me an eye exam but I could not see the chart with any clarity. I guess no one noticed I squinted at the blackboard. Even if I had been seated in the front row I am not sure I could have seen the chart. As it was since I was the tallest girl in my class (and almost the school as far as that goes) I was seated in the back of the class. He also told Dad he had a surprise for him. He said to dad "did you know your girl can only see up close?" Dad looked at me and said "you can't see? Why didn't you tell me?" I did not know what I wasn't seeing!

Again Aunt Gerry was my choice and she came to my rescue. She took me shopping and told Dad I needed some new clothes as I had well out grown all I had. She made an eye appointment with an eye doctor in Springfield and took me to the first appointment. I am sure she paid for some of my new clothes. She said more than once she wished I could wear Frances Mae's size clothing. I would have loved to have her hand me downs. She had really beautiful, and good taste in clothes. But I was much taller and larger than Frances Mae.

I was so happy with my new clothes that I almost forgot about the eye doctor I had seen. Then one day about two weeks later Dad the boys and I went back to Springfield to the eye doctor. He had a pair of glasses for me and I could see the eye chart from across the room. I remembered liking the glasses Aunt Gerry showed me but I did not think anything about it when we put the glasses back and left.

Dad had parked just outside the door of the doctor's office. The boys waited in the car. As we got back to the car I looked up into the sky and there in the sky at noon on an autumn day was a pale moon! I had never seen the moon during the day time. I said "look Dad the moon!" I didn't say it quietly and people along the street was looking at me. Dad grabbed my arm and said "get in the car." Donny laughed like a fool and rolled around in the front seat of the car saying "dumb ole girl the moons up there all the time and you didn't see it, you must be blind." By this time Danny and Jerry were laughing also as I got in the back seat with them. Dad got in the car and said "alright that's enough." It became quiet in the car. Dad stopped and got each one of us a bottle of orange soda and all was good again, and I could see things I never knew were there.

❧ ❧ ❧

Dad was really having a hard time trying to keep his head above water. He worked as much overtime as he could, and depended on us kids to understand. It was hard because he was gone a lot of the time, especially on weekends when he worked in the other miners place. In later years Uncle Pat told me that my Dad did jobs other men would not do just so he could get the overtime. Dad was more and more in despair and a lot of the time he would sit at the table with a cup of coffee and cigarettes and stare at the floor. He did not eat as he should have and lost more weight. After Uncle Buck got killed he hated the mine. I don't think he was afraid he just missed Uncle Buck. It seemed that with Mom and Uncle Bucks deaths he lost interest in almost everything except working and us kids.

❧

In May kids (I found out later it was underprivileged kids that were chosen) from each school district were notified they would be going on a trip after the school term. In June those chosen would be taken to Washington D.C. on a bus trip by Senator Peter F. Mack. Dad thought it would be a good experience for me but I wanted no part of it. Finally Dad told me I had to go. The trip lasted about five days with two or more busloads of kids and chaperones. I can't remember sleeping as we were on the move all the time. We toured the capital and all of the monuments, Arlington cemetery and a beautiful museum. We were taken on a boat ride on the Potomac River where I was introduced to racism.

We ate on the bus going to and from the different places but when we got on the boat that was different. I later realized that the reason we ate on the bus was that if we had eaten in restaurants we would have been separated, the white kid's one place and the Negro kids another. Over time I made friends with several girls on the bus. Two girls Wilma Sauerwein from Bunker Hill and Ruth Oaklely from Hillsboro and I became fast friends and we wrote to one another until I moved to Indiana. There were three Negro girls in the group and they sat in the seat across from us, and we all stayed together.

When we got on the boat the Negro kids and the Negro chaperones were sent to the lower deck. The three of us white girls did not understand. There was a lot of whispering going on and we didn't understand why. It was years later that I fully understood the terrible thing I had witnessed. I had been in a segregation act, and no one asked me what I wanted to do.

❧

I didn't realize it at the time but my Dad was really lonely. He was drinking more and sleeping more when he was not at work. My Dad was strict and used a belt when we disobeyed but he did not abuse any of us. He believed that to spare the rod was to spoil the child and that was the way most families felt the way of the times. He and Don had more head butting but it was mostly because Dad thought one of the boys would get hurt. Dad told Don and me one weekend that he had met someone through a Lonely Hearts club and had begun writing to her. Her name was Melissa Purdue and she lived in Middletown Indiana. Dad talked to us about her and told us where she lived and about her family. She was divorced, had three grown children and a daughter the same age as Don. Later he told us she was coming to Illinois to see if she liked it here.

As I think back now I believe Dad was getting desperate. Mom's family would show up at our home and they always seemed to be looking for something. The women would walk through the rooms look into cabinets and drawers and talk among themselves. They didn't seem to notice I was with them but I took great care to notice what they found to talk about then made the change. One thing the boy's dresser drawers seemed to be a problem so we talked and the boys made certain they put their clothes away neatly. Dad was adamant that they should find nothing to complain about. I believe he was afraid they would take us away from him and I think he was right.

⋰๑ ๖⋰

On September 4, 1951 Aunt Gerry had Dad bring all four of us kids to her house as he went to work. Don and I would be in sophomore class when school started after Labor Day. We had no chores since we moved east of town so we would stay with her until Dad got home from work. When we got to Aunt Gerry and Uncle Pat's home I was in for a surprise, she had dinner for us all and a lovely white cake and a blouse for me. It was my sixteenth birthday.

Later that afternoon I asked Aunt Gerry if I could walk across town to Mom and Dad Richards home. They had recently moved to town. I don't know why I even wanted to talk to Moms family but I now believe that I was looking for validation. It was a beautiful day and I enjoyed the walk. Aunt Gerry kept the boys with her saying it would be good for me to have some time to myself.

When I got to my grandparents' home the place was in chaos. There were strangers on their front porch. Aunt Vesta could be heard hysterical and screaming. Aunt Lena came out of the house, they lived next door west of Mom and Dad Richards, Vesta lived next door on the east side. Aunt Lena told me that Dad Richards had passed away only minutes before and that the doctor was there to see Mom Richards and Vesta. She said Dad Richards body had been taken to the funeral home, the same funeral home where my mother had been. She said I should leave.

I returned to Aunt Gerry sad, my grandfather had passed away on my sixteenth birthday, something I would never forget.

⸎

About the first of Oct. Melissa came to Illinois with her daughter Evelyn, which her mother renamed Taffy (she had lovely blonde hair) in order to tell us apart when talking to us. At that time Dad told us they were getting married. On October 27, 1951 Dad married Melissa at the Edinburg Christian Church. Melissa's daughter and son-in-law Phyllis and Lester Black were their witnesses.

We kids liked having a woman in the house, we went to school came home to supper then we four kids cleaned up the kitchen, did our homework and went to bed. Melissa's daughter did not go to school with us but had her school work sent to her from Indiana and her mom schooled her. Melissa was afraid in the country and Dad began to look for a house in town, but they couldn't seem to find one they both agreed on.

Melissa and Taffy went back to Indiana several times. Each time when they got back I think it was harder for them to come to the country. Holidays came and went. We were snowed in that winter several times with our road closed and it seemed to cause Melissa to panic to think she could not get to town. One time when we were snowed in the family even walked to Edinburg which was five or six miles, for nothing really. We ate hamburgers, got a few groceries and walked back home. A half mile of the road was blocked, but the main road was open. It was a warm sunny day with a lot of snow banks.

Years later I wondered how terrible it would have been if the wind had come up and blizzard conditions had started while we were gone. I can't think how terrible it must have been to want to go to town so badly as to walk that far in snow for no real reason. We were used to being snowed in during the winter. Melissa made Dad park the car about a half mile up the road so we could get out if we got snowed in again. The road was always plowed out in time for Dad to go to work. We kids would walk in the field to the neighbor's house and meet the school bus. They kept house hunting to no avail. There just did not seem to be a house in Edinburg that suited Melissa, and Taffy was very unhappy, she wanted to go back to Indiana.

January 1952 Dad quit his job at the coal mine and told us kids not to tell anyone we were leaving. We packed our clothes, left most of our personal things and household furnishings, although I took Mom's sewing machine from the cabinet. Dad told me he would make a cabinet for me. I had taken Home Economics for two extra classes for two years and made my own clothes. I could also make shirts for the boys and mend our clothes. Almost all of our things were shipped to Middletown Indiana. I could hardly stand to think about leaving although Mom's family was making it harder for us all the time. It had gotten better since Dad had remarried. Dad told me that if I was OK with the move then the boys would be, somehow I made it OK.

Dad got a job on the railroad through Mellissa's brother in law Floyd. Melisa and her sister Lillian married brothers, Rufus and Floyd. We kids started to school and I was able to walk the little boys to their school. I was a duck out of water in a large school. We all made friends and Rufus, Taffy's father came every Sunday morning and took all five of us kids to the Nazarene Church where he and Floyd, Lillian and their family attended. Everyone was good to us except Melissa's two sons. They let Dad know they did not like us living in their house. Melissa had gotten the house in the divorce settlement. Rufus Jr. lived with his Dad and John whom we met once or twice joined the service and we never saw him again.

In late February Dad got laid off from the railroad. Melissa said I had to quit school and get a job. I worked part time as a waitress after school for about two weeks, but she meant a full time job. She found me a job in Anderson keeping house and taking care of a baby for her niece and her family, they had two other children. I stayed there from Sunday evening till about noon on Saturday when they brought me home. It was real hard work and I missed the little boys so much I didn't think I could stand it. Dad said I would have to do it until he found another job.

Don must have thought it was a lark not to go to school, because he quit and no one knew it! Dad made lunches for the kids in the morning and Don walked the boys to school then went to the river for the rest of the day!! When school was out he would be waiting for the boys and walk them home. In later years Danny said he knew Don was not going to school but he had been sworn to secrecy.

When I came home after a few weeks of working and I never knew how much I made as the people paid Melissa, I realized things were not good between Dad and Melissa. Don did not like her anymore and he really liked her when she came to Illinois. He now referred to her as Momma Lissy but the biggest scare was Jerry. He wouldn't talk, and I saw bruises that no one could or would explain. Finally one weekend when I got home Melissa said she had made arrangements for me to stay permanently with the people I was working for. I was not to come back. Dad didn't seem to have any say in the matter. I worked about two weeks and got sick, I couldn't eat or sleep I knew something was wrong.

The people took me home on a Friday (I think) and I was in for the shock of my life. Melissa had laid the law down to Dad and the boys!

Danny told me she was whipping Jerry a lot, for very little reason. I had never been so angry in my life. I jumped Melissa (literally) and asked why she was whipping Jerry. She gave me a short answer, something to the effect that she could if she wanted to! Dad and Don hauled me off her, but I told her if she laid a hand on my two little brothers again I would kill her. I think she knew I meant it. She tried to act different after that and she tried to be sweet when Dad was around, but she was too little too late. When Dad was gone looking for work she was her same old mean self, even dumb country kids are hard to fool. Her daughter could do no wrong, she was spoiled and did not like the attention the little boys got, however small it was.

I just kept the boys out of their way. Dad would not let me go back to work. I thought to myself that he had a plan but he did not discuss it with me. The weather was not that bad so I made sandwiches for all four of us and we went to the river with Don after school and on weekends. We did this for about two weeks. Don had dug out a cave under some tree roots on the river bank and had himself a nice little dry cave. Unless someone walked right up to the opening no one knew it was there. Don told us of people fishing very close by and they did not know he was anywhere around. He loved this game of intrigue.

The first of April Dad and Melissa separated. We had nowhere to go, and only Dads unemployment money. Melissa's sister Lillian and husband Floyd offered us the loft over their garage. They had four children at home, three in school and a very small home. We were grateful for the offer. Also Melissa had another sister Jo and her husband who lived in another town. She and Lillian loaned us things like army cots to sleep on, blankets and linens and other things we needed. Everything we had shipped to Indiana stayed with Melissa. All we had were our clothes, not even our suitcases to put the clothes in, paper sacks would do for us. I managed to take my sewing machine with me.

We had a small stove to cook on and for heat. Dad partitioned off a corner with a blanket for us to dress. About a week after our exile Melissa came to the loft to look around, I do not think she was happy to see we were doing so well. After all we did have food and a bed each.

She and Dad left to talk. Dad stayed with her for a short time to try to work things out. She wanted to get back with Dad but she did not want us kids around even in her sister's garage. When Dad came back he told us we were going home to Illinois.

All of us liked Melissa's sisters and their families, so we took pictures of everyone, I was glad I had taken our old camera that someone had given us. We prepared to leave. I believe Lillian, Floyd, Jo and her husband and Melissa's ex-husband Rufus were sincere when they said they wished things had worked out for Dad and Melissa. I believe it would have if it had not been for the four of us kids. I admire Dad for not leaving us somewhere or putting us up for adoption, but he promised Mom not to split us up. I don't know what I would have done if I had lost Danny and Jerry.

Part V

13

Return to Illinois

On the 29th of April Dad bought bus tickets, loaded us kids and himself onto the bus and we all came back to Illinois. At 1:30 am we got to Uncle Sharkey (Elmer) and Aunt Tory-Bells home in Hillsboro, they did not know we were coming. Aunt Tory did not have beds for all of us so I suggested pallets on the floor would be great. Their two girls were the same age as my two little brothers. I ended upstairs, with all four kids on pallets on the floor. Donny bunked in the same room as our cousin Bob, he was about my age. The girls and my brothers giggled half the night. Danny was becoming a comedian just like his big brother.

Early the next morning I woke and slipped from the room and down the stairs to help Aunt Tory in the kitchen. When I opened the stairway door into the large dining room I was amazed that the table was set for both families, this was five extra people for a total of twelve people. Aunt Tory's family consisted of wife, husband, and son Bob. He and Uncle Sharkey were both crippled from a pickup truck and tractor trailer wreck which had taken the life of an older son. Also making up the family were two girls Nancy and Rita, and the twin boys Garry and Larry who were born the same time as my sister Shirley.

I walked into the kitchen to find my aunt at the big iron cook stove where there were skillets of meat, milk gravy and an enormous pan of tall biscuits. The most precious thing in that kitchen was the big honest smile on Aunt Tory's face. She enveloped me into those great loving arms and I felt so safe, a feeling I had not felt since my mother had last hugged me. One would never have known that we were unexpected company. We were made welcome from the time we walked into the house and all the time we were there.

Don and I did dishes after breakfast and all we could talk about was how good the food was, it was cooking like Mom used to do. Dad had helped Uncle Sharkey do the milking and they had gone off to finish the chores. Rita, Nancy, Danny and Jerry came through the kitchen, grabbed biscuits and outside they went. I started to scold the boys but didn't they were happier than I had seen them for a long time. Bob was a ham radio operator so he and Don went off to do radio stuff. I was left with my precious aunt. We talked of things she remembered about my Mom, garden, canning; just wonderful memories. Then we went upstairs to see what we could do about sleeping arrangements.

Aunt Tory was a large lady and they didn't use the upstairs much because they had plenty of room downstairs. We thought we had the sleeping all arranged until night came. We had planned so dad could use a bed in one of the rooms upstairs and Danny, Don, Jerry and I would sleep on the floor in another room. Sounds smooth until Bob suggested that they put an army cot that was in one of the upstairs rooms in his room for Don. He wanted to teach Don to be a ham radio operator. They talked to people all over the country on the radio all night.

Both girls piped up with wanting to sleep where Danny, Jerry and I slept. They set up such a howl that I told Aunt Tory it was fine with me. (The more the merrier.) Then the two little twins decided if their sisters could go upstairs so could they. They began to cry. Aunt Tory was adamant that they could not because of the stairs. I told her I would sleep in front of the door and take the children to the bathroom at night or get water for them so they did not go downstairs alone. After the first night we took water up stairs with us. The bathroom was a little house out back and I took the kids out two at a time. It was strange that I had no fear at all of the dark in the country but I had been afraid in town. It was so good to go to sleep to the sound of night birds again. Dad was glad to take one of the girls room downstairs and we all settled in.

Dad tried to find work but most of the farmers had hired their workers already. I suggested to Dad I could work in a restaurant in town to help out. So Dad borrowed Uncle Sharkey's truck and took me to work and came and got me when the shift was over. When Dad could not get work right away he went to Uncle Sharkey and Aunt Tory for advice. They wanted him to go back to Indiana and try to work something out with Melissa, they did not believe in divorce only as a last resort. They did not believe in mistreating children and would not let us kids go back unless she agreed to treat us well. Obviously Dad could not move on with our lives until his affairs were settled. They told Dad that the four of us kids would stay with them so there would be no problem.

Dad left and Uncle Sharkey took me to work. This worked out well until the owners put me on the evening shift, then I did not get off work until about 10 pm. This was a hardship for Uncle Sharkey. Aunt Tory took me aside and she convinced me that with gardens and canning I could be more help at home than working. I couldn't stand feeling like we were sponging off people. Don and I both knew how to garden take care of chickens and milk the cows. We were all ready to do the milking one evening when Uncle Sharkey said he did not allow strangers in his barn. He talked gruff but was a real kitten. His left arm had been broken so badly in the truck wreck that it was pinned and permanently bent at the elbow. There Don and I stood with milk buckets in hand and not allowed in the barn! He suggested we could feed the hog's ear corn if we were of a mind. After that I helped in the house and Don fed the hogs.

When Uncle Sharkey passed the six little kids in the yard on his way to the barn he would always tell them "you little nubbins have to be quiet or you'll scare my cows", which always caused Nancy and Rita to yell and scream at the tops of their lungs. Uncle Sharkey would just grin and stroll off to the barn. I wonder if he would not have been disappointed if the kids had kept quiet.

That summer will always be one of my favorites. We got our work done in the very early part of the day, sometimes before breakfast, since chores were done before eating. Aunt Tory would have bread dough set to rise and dinner started by the time the breakfast dishes were done. Nancy, Rita, Danny, Jerry and I did all the dishes. The kids worked well together in the kitchen even if they scrambled when they were away from Aunt Tory and me. Aunt Tory told us she would "forget" how to wash dishes when we were gone and her girls told her they would gladly teach her again.

After dinner the routine was always the same, Uncle Sharkey would listen to a baseball game on the radio and nap, Bob and Don were on the ham radio. Uncle Sharkey's farm was owned between him and another man with a hired man that worked for Uncle Sharkey. Aunt Tory took all the rest of us out on the big wrap around front porch and read to us. I loved hearing her read even the children's books. Each child would have their own folded blanket to lie on. First thing we knew all six children would be asleep, and then it was my time with Aunt Tory. She reminded me so much of Mom, I cry when I think of that time. They did not look alike, Mom was slender and tall and Aunt Tory was short and very round. However both women knew what was important in life. Aunt Tory talked to me a lot about my parent's and I learned or figured out a lot of things such as more details of my parent's relationship with Mom's parents and why Mom was so partial to Aunt Tory over her sisters. Many years later Rita would send me papers and letters that Aunt Tory had that would explain so much. Aunt Tory was a true friend to my mother and to me.

Whichever one of the six sleeping children opened their eyes first made sure the other five were awake and off they went. Their favorite time was for all of us to go to the creek to hunt turtles. I have always wondered where so many came from. The turtles had to be removed from the creek where the ducks were because they ate the feet off the baby ducks! Whatever turtles we caught Uncle Sharkey would dress and they would freeze the meat until we had enough for a meal. Some of the turtles were quite large. Aunt Tory would bake the turtle meat in the oven and it was so good. A far cry from my brother's frog legs on the creek bank cooking.

14

A New Start

In September Dad came home from Indiana one afternoon. It wasn't that far from town and he came walking up the drive with an old beat up suitcase not one of our new ones. I almost knew things were not the way he wanted by the way he walked. That night all of us were sent to bed early with a request from Aunt Tory for me to read to the kids. The three grownups talked far into the night. A few days later Uncle Sharkey took Dad to the bus station and he went up north to their sister Edith's home in Lovington to look for work. At Dad's request Uncle Sharkey had asked around about work in their area and there did not seem to be any.

Dad was gone a couple of weeks and one day Uncle Sharkey called Don and me in after the mail had gone. I just knew something terrible was wrong. Aunt Tory was crying and Uncle Sharkey seemed to have trouble talking. He said that Dad had found a job and a house for us and he was coming to get us. I was scared, I felt so safe with Aunt Tory.

It was so hard to say goodbye when Aunt Edith and Dad came to get us. Early on the morning of September 29, 1952 Aunt Tory and Uncle Sharkey packed us with all kinds of good things and we left to go live near Sullivan I was seventeen years old. Dad got a job working for Chuck Sanders. I hated to leave the safety of Aunt Tory's arms and go into the unknown again. The last time had been terrifying in Indiana. As we prepared to leave Aunt Tory told me if things did not work out we were always welcome to return to her. Just knowing this gave me the knowledge and stability to think I could take care of myself and the boys.

Dad borrowed Aunt Edith's car until he could buy one. Don went to work doing chores for a Mr. Wiley, who had broken his leg that autumn. We started the boys in school at Jonathan Creek and Pat Sanders hired me to help her with housework and babysit with their two boys Stanley and Greg. Then Chuck hired Don to haul corn in from the fields. Don took his wages in the form of a car that Chuck had for sale. I went over to Mr. and Mrs. Wiley and asked for Don's old job. Mr. Wiley was not at all responsive to a girl doing his chores. He asked me how I would get the baby pigs to go in at night as they could get out if they wanted to. I told him I would close the gate on the sow and she would call them in. I got the job.

I would get the boys ready for school and when I saw the bus coming I would leave and walk across the field to the Wiley farm and do their chores, they had sheep and hogs but no cattle or horses. I did the chores again in the evening just after the boys got home from school. We had to trust the boys to behave while I was gone; they did and seemed to enjoy their responsibility. This worked well since the sheep were free range and Mr. Wiley set the chore time. We all three were working! During the day I made the house as clean and fixed up as I could always hoping Mom would have approved. I thought of her so much and missed her unbelievably.

Chuck told Dad about an Amish sale near Arthur so we went in Don's car; however Dad drove with Don co-piloting. Don never tired of explaining all the wonderful gadgets on his car to anyone who would listen and Danny and Jerry were all ears. We bought several pieces of furniture which Chuck hauled home for us and Dad bought several boxes of canned fruit and vegetables. He also bought some quilts.

Our home was coming together. Dad put Mom's sewing machine head in a table cabinet for me and although it was still a treadle machine

I was most happy when I was making curtains or sewing something for the family or making skirts for the sinks. I made a dressing table for my bedroom with a skirt around it which turned out very well. We went to several sales that fall and made good buys. Then I lost my job, Mr. Wiley got his cast off and I was out of work. I told him if he knew of anyone who needed help to let me know.   Not long after that Mr. Kirby and his two daughters came by one evening. They lived down by the river south of us. Mr. Kirby said he had talked to Mr. Wiley and that I was looking for work. He said the shoe factory in Sullivan was hiring. Dad took me into town and I put in an application. I was hired on at the Brown Shoe factory in January 1953 and I paid to ride back and forth to work with Mr. Kirby and Lavone who worked there also.

The Kirby family went to the Baptist church in Sullivan and invited the boys and me to go with them. I was grateful as the boys were getting harder to handle. They wanted to do whatever Don did and Don was doing some pretty dumb things, like working on his car.

I was working some Saturdays in the fitting room but Mr. Kirby who worked in the kitchen and Lavone who worked in the cutting room didn't, this meant Dad had to take me to work and come get me even though he also worked Saturdays. Dad thought that if I knew how to drive I could borrow Don's car on Saturday and also grocery shop on the way home. This sounded reasonable so Don began my driving lessons. For what seemed like weeks I had to practice driving in the drive way and had to stay inside the lines Don had marked for me.   On a Saturday afternoon it was a usual event for the four of us to go to Cooks Mills or to Allenville to the grocery store buy ice cream and orange soda and enjoy an afternoon of soda drinks, Danny and Jerry lived for Saturday. We had gone to Allenville to the store and on the way home Don declared that I was ready to drive on the road with his tutelage. I was nervous because I knew that if I made any mistakes my lessons would be over. Don stopped the car and we exchanged drivers. The fool had parked on a hill and as I was trying to get the car in gear (it was a stick shift) Don was yelling at me and I was so nervous, it rolled back down the hill and into the ditch. The fender was bent and so ended my driving career for a while. About this time Dad bought a car and he took over the driving lessons.

❧

I met someone special at the shoe factory, he worked in the same department that I did. Bernice and Clovis Franklin went to the Baptist Church and when I started working at the shoe factory I was in the same department as she was. She made it a point of introducing me to Garrett Burtcheard. Sometime after that he asked me to go to a movie, however I declined, I couldn't go. I had too much to do at home and was working Saturdays so that Saturday night was when I cleaned house. Dad took the boys to town to a movie and he would do our weekly shopping for groceries. Garrett and I talked at work but I didn't think of our relationship as a serious one.

Bernice and I talked and I told her I wanted to get an education but I could not afford to quit work to go to high school. I read about learning to be a nurse through home schooling. I signed up and started paying my tuition and thought I was on my way to a career in nursing after all I had spent most of my life patching up and doctoring my brothers. I did my home work late into the night and got good grades. Then it was time to go to a hospital to apply for on the job training. During inventory shutdown at the shoe factory I was going to apply at Taylorville hospital. The boys and Dad gave me their blessing. I had hoped to stay with Mom Richards although she had moved in with Vesta and had sold her home. Dad was not in favor of this but finally agreed on the condition that I had to pay room and board.

I got all kinds of bad news. The hospital at Taylorville would not even consider an interview so Dad took me to the two hospitals in Springfield. I was told that no hospital would accept a home school nursing program. At the same time Vesta and Mom Richards informed me it would be a hardship for me to stay with them. They had not helped my Mom so where I had gotten the idea they would help me I will never know, but I think Dad was aware. It was wishful thinking I guess. As I got in touch with other families at Edinburg they all acted like they were glad to hear from us.

The nursing school tried to sue me for not finishing their course. Bernice knew how disappointed I was and told me not to send them anymore money, instead she sent me to the States Attorney Joseph Munch in our county. I gathered every piece of paper I had from the school and very scared I went to the courthouse. I had never even been in a courthouse before. Mr. Munch was a very quiet soft spoken man and put me at ease. He said he would send a letter to the school on my behalf but for me not to send any more money. The threats stopped and I never heard from the school again. My dreams of becoming a nurse died.

Suddenly the Edinburg folks were interested in us again. One Sunday Vesta, Mom Richards, Ronny, Uncle Frank, Aunt Sina and Shirley arrived unexpected. I had worked at the shoe factory a half day on Saturday and cleaned house good Saturday afternoon and night. Dad had dinner ready when the boys and I got home from church. We were just finishing the dishes when the strange car drove into the yard. I was glad to see Mom's family, why I don't know but I was. Silly ole me!

I was so thankful that I had the house cleaning done. Sometimes I would have to finish cleaning on Sunday afternoon if I had worked all day on Saturday. I managed to keep the laundry done during the week. We had area rugs I shook but since we did not have a vacuum cleaner all the floors had to be mopped and waxed. I had those floors shining. There were a few tense moments when the company first arrived, we didn't know what to expect and I knew we would not stand for any nonsense from any of them. Donny and I were old enough to voice our opinions and we would fight if we had to, no one was going to take the boys from us and that was what came to my mind.

I had baked a cake the night before and I remember trying to remember exactly how Mom served refreshments. Dad made coffee and the visit turned out well. I believe this was so because we no longer needed help from them. Of course there was a lot of discussion after they left. That summer we had several visits from Mom's family, Uncle Charlie and Aunt Lena, Norma Jean and Freddy came several times.

Of all the family the visits from Vesta and her current husband or boyfriend were the weirdest. She came to show her latest acquisition as if her life should be an example. Each man she brought was a grade lower than the last. She was not improving her life just another bar fly. None of us were impressed least of all Dad. It was hard for him not to show his dislike for her. No one ever asked until many years later where we had gone or what we did those two missing years that we were gone. It had been as if they had come for a visit just last week. I think that it was because we no longer needed help and it appeared to them we were doing well for ourselves. As a family we needed to prove that to Mom's family. I tried to remember how Mom kept things so neat and clean.

The boys accumulated a zoo by the time we had been at Sullivan a very short time. Dogs rabbits a kitten or two and some pigeons from somewhere. The first Christmas Dad, Don and I pooled our money and bought the boys used bicycles. The kids seemed to be truly happy and they were doing well in school. I talked Dad into letting me buy the boys jeans instead of overalls and slippers instead of high top shoes for school. It was a hard sell but finally we wore him down on one condition that they keep their shirt tails tucked in. They were so happy with jeans and cowboy shirts that I was glad I had argued with Dad for them. Then we began to receive invitations from Edinburg for us to visit. Dad was nervous but we wanted to see Shirley so we went at Aunt Sina's invitation. I was always particular about the way the boys looked. I made them wear their church clothes white shirts, dress pants, shined shoes and good manners. Dad began to relent and the boys now wore jeans and shirts to Edinburg to visit.

Don worked pretty steady and bought himself a shotgun. Dad had taught us some of how to use a rifle when Don and I were eleven and twelve years old. However we were not allowed to touch it unless he was there. Don and Dad did practice shooting behind the machinery barn. I shot the shotgun once. Don told me to brace myself against the machinery shed. I did, the shotgun kicked and my shoulder felt like it was broken. My ears rang for a long time. That was the end of my wanting to shoot the shotgun. I much preferred the .22 rifle. I wasn't a good shot but I did like to shoot.

Don went hunting pretty often but didn't have much to show for it. Danny and Jerry were driving me crazy to go with Don. I was not about to let them go without me. When we got to a huge brush pile Don was just certain there were rabbits in it, since there were rabbit tracks all around so that made sense. The little boys although they were eleven and thirteen (they were still little in my eyes) and I stood well back.

Don became desperate circling the brush pile. Finally he turned to me and said, "Evelyn climb up on top and jump up and down and they will run out." Without thinking it through I said, "You are not going to shoot are you?" "Naw not until they are clear." I climbed to the top and jumped up and down, the rabbits ran out and Don shot, into the bottom of the brush pile, and I didn't think that far from my feet. Well so much for trust and we still didn't get a rabbit.

❧ↄ৩

In the spring Don went mushroom hunting and wanted the boys to go with him. In order for them to go I had to go with them. We went to the timber south of our home and everyone began hunting mushrooms, except for me, I was afraid of snakes and watched for them. In my blundering around I stepped on a patch of mushrooms and Don became furious, once again I was the dumb ole girl of old. I didn't find any mushrooms but I also made certain I did not find any snakes.

A NEW START

✑✑

On October 4, 1954 I started dating Garrett. Dad and the boys liked him on sight. I had talked to Bernice and she spoke highly of Garrett telling me what a nice person he was. The boys wanted to come with Garrett and I, reminding me they had gone to a school dance and this was no different. So we took them on dates for hamburgers. When the circus came to Sullivan Garrett took us all. It was our first ever circus and the boys talked about it for weeks. When Garrett came to pick me up they would ask if he saw such and such at the circus. The boys were growing up fast.

Danny Jerry and I were baptized into the Baptist Church on the 22nd of November, 1954 by Rev. Richard Krell. I stayed a Baptist until after I was married then I joined the church Garrett and his mother went to The Disciples of Christ Christian Church.

Mumps were all over the county Garrett had them the winter before. Don, Danny and Jerry had them all at the same time. Doctor Phillip Best became our doctor and friend. He was very concerned when he was told that Jerry had previously had rheumatic fever. I was supposed to keep them all quiet!! For once Don was not the culprit. He had driven a tractor all day and Dad said he was sick when they went in for dinner but would not stay home in the afternoon. The mumps went down on him and he was truly one sick puppy.

Danny had a light case while Jerry was very sick. As they improved Danny became a real monkey. Jerry or Don would yell for me to come help them and there would be Danny grinning from ear to ear. I had taken time off from the shoe factory to take care of them and could hardly wait to go back to work.

We learned that two of the neighbor boys also had the mumps, Jack Leonard and Marvin Kirby. Each family would buy comic books then I would take the ones we had to Jack, Jack's to Marvin and bring Marvin's back to my brothers. When Doctor Best was told how I was keeping the boys quiet he said I was most likely a carrier since I had not taken the mumps and I didn't.

Our paternal grandfather passed away, he was 85 years old. All I could remember of him was that he was a very mean, hard person and Granny was afraid of him. He remarried after Granny died and his second wife didn't want Granddad to have anything to do with his children. I don't think Mom liked him but I can't remember any of the family saying much about him one way or the other.

✌︎∽✇∽

The time was passing and the boys were growing up, I managed to keep them in Sunday school and Church. Garrett and I continued to date and Garrett asked me to marry him. I told him I wanted to marry him but I would like to wait until Jerry was a little older, thirteen. Don was finding many things to do that I did not approve of. One such venture was the making of home brew, there were two of Don's friends involved Roger and James.

Don and Jack also tried their hand at being car mechanics which landed them in the ditch and a corn field. They had repaired something on the car that required removing the steering wheel. Putting the wheel back on was another matter. They were driving north of the road from Jack's house known as the county line road. Don was driving and the steering wheel came off in his hands! He tried to give the wheel to Jack but Jack did not want it or know what to do with it. They ended up in the corn field!

✌︎∽✇∽

In the fall of 1955 I took the boys for an overnight stay with Uncle Charlie and Aunt Lena they had asked us to come for the weekend. I had gotten my driver's license and Dad said we could go. I was surprised since one afternoon Dad had sent me to go pick up the boys at school and on the way a bumble bee got in the car and flew into my face. I drove off the road and took out three or four fence posts at Powell's farm. Mr. Powell and Dad did not get mad and Mr. Powell wouldn't let me pay for the repairs. Mr. Powell teased me every time he saw me about taking out his fence. The boys never passed the area that they didn't remind me I had "gone in the ditch and tore out the fence." When we got to Edinburg we found Uncle Charlie's household in an uproar. Norma Jean and Jr. Zini had eloped. Uncle Charlie was crushed he had envisioned his little girl getting married in a white dress and veil.

❧ ❧

I told Dad that Garrett had asked me to marry him but I did not think the boys were ready for me to leave. Jerry would be thirteen in March. Dad reminded me that he would be the age I was when Mom died and that I would still be around to help them. He told me I should accept Garrett's proposal. Dad and the boys liked Garrett very much. Christmas 1955 Garrett gave me a diamond engagement ring and a beautiful blue velvet quilted robe from an exclusive dress shop. I had never owned anything like it, it was so beautiful. This was my last Christmas at home with the boys and I tried to make it special. With Dad's permission I bought the boys B-B guns. Of course we had many, many more Christmas's but the last in many ways. The boys were growing up so fast and would be on their own soon. It was time for me to get on with my life.

I took Garrett to meet the Edinburg family and was not at all surprised that they liked him too. The women doted on him especially Aunt Sina after she found out he liked grape pie. Uncles Charlie and Uncle Frank told Dad that Garrett was a good man.

On the day Garrett and I got married January 21, 1956 my only family was Dad, Danny and Jerry. Don had enlisted in the Marines and at 4 am I had taken Don and two of his friends Chuck and James to Decatur to catch the train for boot camp in California. Relations between Dad and Don had become strained, Don was very head strong. Dad was advised that the service would be good for Don so when Don approached Dad he signed the papers allowing him to join the

Marines. The Edinburg folk begged off coming to my wedding saying the weather was too bad. Almost all of Garrett's family was there except one brother in law that could not get leave from the Air Force.

Don had left his car for me to drive while he was gone to the Marines. So the very hour I was being married Don was on his way to Camp Pendleton, CA. Jerry and Dad were in Dad's car and Danny and I were in Don's car on the way to the church. Danny was pretty quiet and finally said, "Sis do you have butterflies in your stomach?" I said that I didn't, to which he said, "Boy I sure do." I don't think slick roads had anything to do with butterflies since none of us cared for large gatherings.

My life would change, I still had the boys to sort of look after. Dad met someone and two years later moved to Decatur. He started working in a factory where he got hurt and eventually had back surgery that did not go well. On February 22, 1957 I had a baby boy that my teen age brothers thought hung the moon and it was a pleasure to see them holding the tiny bundle. As the boys grew older they followed in Don's footsteps and joined the service, but they joined the Air Force. They made lives for themselves in Texas after they got out of the service. Danny became a policeman and Jerry a truck driver.

When Danny and Jerry wanted to join the service I used the text books Garrett's family had used to help them get their GED. Mom Burtcheard encouraged me to get my GED. She took care of Rick so I could take the tests. Then I took classes as they were available at the local high school. I had had to quit school and always felt sort of lost because I did not feel smart and after I got married I still wanted more education.

After Rick got out of high school I wanted him to go to college. That was not what he wanted so I took his basic classes and could not get enough school. I went to Lake Land College, St-Mary-of the Woods through a program where I worked at General Electric, the WED program and Eastern University. I got two degrees plus several ongoing classes in computer and a continuous writing course. I finally satisfied the longing for an education I had always wanted. And I realized I could write while taking writing classes.

Don lived in California but he died young as the result of an accident on an off shore oil rig in the Texas gulf and years of ongoing surgeries. Danny passed away with cancer. Jerry and Shirley's deaths were unknown. The rest of my life I remained in rural Moultrie County with Garrett, and my horses. Our son Rick and his wife lived a few miles from us until his death at age 54. Dad and the boys are all gone now and I am the only survivor of Christian Forty.

CPSIA information can be obtained
at www.ICGtesting.com
Printed in the USA
FFOW01n0902150616
25033FF

9 781478 773696